# CHINESE INTELLECTUALS AND THE GOSPEL

Samuel Ling and Stacey Bieler, Editors

CHINA HORIZON

P.O. Box 2209, San Gabriel, CA 91778

HORIZON MINISTRIES CANADA

201-745 Broadway, Vancouver, BC V5Z 4J7

Distributed by

P U B L I S H I N G

P.O. BOX 817 • PHILLIPSBURG • NEW JERSEY 08865-0817

China Horizon, San Gabriel 91778
Horizon Ministries Canada, Vancouver
© 1999 by China Horizon and Horizon Ministries
Canada
All rights reserved. Published 1999.
ISBN 1-892-63204-7

# CONTENTS

Chinese intellectuals have been searching for an all-comprehensive ideology to guide China's cultural transformation since 1900. Christianity was unable to provide biblical and relevant answers to the despairing intellectuals during the May Fourth Period (1915-1927). Eventually, many Chinese students turned to Communism. The Tiananmen Square tragedy of June 4, 1989, symbolized another turning point, when Chinese intellectuals again despaired over finding an answer to China's problems. Samuel Ling, president of China Horizon, believes that Christians seeking to reach Chinese intellectuals need to be equipped to share a biblical worldview and philosophy of history.

## PART I

## UNDERSTANDING CHINESE INTELLECTUALS: HISTORICAL AND CULTURAL BACKGROUND

The history of the interaction between the gospel and Chinese society highlights the importance of understanding Chinese cultural dynamics. Jonathan Chao, president of China Ministries International, gives a historical overview of the entry of Christianity into China since the seventh century A.D. Chao shows how China's political dynamics, especially state control over religion and ideology, have been the foremost obstacle in evangelizing the Chinese people. Since confrontational approaches among Chinese intellectuals have not proven effective, Christians need to seek more gracious techniques, that, while preserving the integrity of the biblical message, will reach Chinese intellectuals where they are.

Throughout history China's intellectuals have walked the tightrope of serving their rulers while providing social and political critique. The leaders in China today are caught between needing the intellectuals' technological contributions and fearing their critique of injustice and corruption. Stacey Bieler, a veteran PRC ministry worker and former staff member with InterVarsity Christian Fellowship, looks at this tension that has shaped the Chinese intellectuals' mindset and critical approach.

The push for modernization in the 1980s gave Chinese intellectuals a window of opportunity to influence policy-making while voicing their dissenting views. While in previous generations intellectuals had depended on vertical relationships with high-ranking officials, the need for experts to cooperate with the government in economic and technological reforms allowed intellectuals to make horizontal connections. Disunity among the generations of intellectuals, however, became a major factor in the failure of the Spring 1989 student demonstrations.

During the decade of reform (1980s), six major schools of thought arose among Chinese intellectuals. Some looked to traditional Chinese thought, while others looked to the West for answers to China's needs. Several groups focused their interest on the study of Christianity. Liu Xiaofeng provides a glimpse into the more open atmosphere in the years leading up to the Tiananmen Square tragedy.

The People's Liberation Army crushed student protesters at Tiananmen Square on June 4, 1989. The pain and despair of the students, as well as of sympathetic Chinese in Hong Kong, found expression in these poems. This collection gives the reader a glimpse into the deep angst of mainland Chinese intellectuals in their search for a new social order and into their openness to Christian motifs.

Ping Cheung Lo, ethics professor at Hong Kong Baptist University, sparked a significant debate when he published this essay in Hong Kong's *Christian Times*. "China's Apolloses" refers to mainland intellectuals who are sympathetic toward Christianity and who encourage it as an ideology to shape China's future. Some have even adopted the Christian faith personally. Like Apollos in the Acts of the Apostles, they are learned, eloquent, and competent in debate, but do not have a complete understanding of God's truth. Yet these Chinese "Apolloses" promise to become the most prominent spokespeople for Christianity in China's academic circles. Lo raises a pertinent question: Will Hong Kong's theologians be eclipsed in the process?

The Communist Revolution of 1949 ushered in a period when religious studies were banned from both church and university. Since 1976, scholars have begun questioning their Maoist assumptions, and many have turned to investigate Christian thought and culture. These professors of philosophy, history, foreign languages, and social sciences are mostly appreciative of Christianity's potential contribution to the future development of Chinese culture. A few have become Christians. Mainland Chinese professor Chun-fu Chen and medical ethicist Edwin Hui of Regent College (Vancouver. B.C.) provide a comprehensive framework for understanding these "scholars in mainland China studying Christianity" (SMSCs) as an alternative to Ping Cheung Lo's designation, "China's Apolloses."

## PART II

## REACHING CHINESE INTELLECTUALS: STRATEGIES AND MODELS FOR EVANGELISM AND DISCIPLESHIP

Ling examines various approaches to PRC ministry currently undertaken by Christians in the West. He then looks at the intellectual and theological issues that PRC ministry workers face.

Rawson analyzes the worldview of mainland Chinese, including their social networks and value systems. She then provides suggestions for presenting the gospel without uncritically promoting Western culture.

When does the Holy Spirit work the new birth in a person? When does a person exercise faith and repentance? When does a person gain assurance of salvation? Regeneration, faith, assurance, and assimilation into the church are seen as both processes and mysterious workings of God. Ling implicitly challenges the assumption that all conversions take place at one moment in time.

Personal conversations with PRCs provide insight into their minds and souls. Topics for conversation include marriage and family, politics, and economics. Suggestions for Bible study passages and resources, such as movies, are included in this practical guide to deeper friendships with Chinese scholars.

The non-return of Chinese students sent abroad is an irritant to China's modernization. Many complex factors - personal, practical, family, and political - affect Chinese students' decisions whether to return to China, to stay in North America, or to find a third alternative. Bieler encourages sensitivity and understanding of this "migration of talent" as we listen to our friends agonize over their decisions.

Chinese intellectuals who have received Christ need a vision of God's kingdom in order to lead lives of obedience and service. They need to learn about servant-leadership, Christian community, and responsible involvement in society based on hope in God. Resources and a potential structure for small group study are included.

# PREFACE

This volume of essays on Chinese intellectuals has been prepared for those who love and pray for China. It is offered to those who love the gospel and pray for its impact among the Chinese people. It is presented with appreciation for our colleagues who have labored in this exciting and intriguing field, and offers new perspectives to understand our task of evangelism and discipleship among PRCs (mainland Chinese scholars and students studying in the west).

Traditionally, western Christians, as well as overseas Chinese Christians, have understood evangelism in terms of an interpersonal process of proclamation. Whether through special meetings featuring itinerant evangelists, or through one-on-one, canned presentations of the gospel, the gospel is proclaimed in order that individuals can come to a point of profession of faith, or a "prayer to receive Christ." We will call this "Model A" evangelism. Its strength is focus of energy, and an unswerving commitment to accomplish the Great Commission of our Lord Jesus Christ. Its popular use among evangelicals worldwide will continue into the twenty-first century.

Since the 1970s, however, both western and overseas Chinese Christians have added "Model B" as a supplement to "Model A." This newer approach emphasizes the need to nurture those who make commitments to receive Christ, and includes many multi-session programs to teach a new convert how to pray, read the Bible, give a personal testimony of their new-found faith, and become incorporated into the church. This is "Model B," the "discipleship" model of evangelism. It seeks to overcome some of the weaknesses in "Model A," and has helped to sustain an entire generation of western and overseas Chinese converts in the first years of their walk with Christ. It has effectively stemmed the tide of attrition among new believers.

The coming of PRCs to study in the West in the 1980s has presented an unforeseen challenge to the western and the overseas Chinese church. Many of mainland China's brightest minds have received the ministry of hospitality and pre-evangelism from western Christians (especially in the pioneering period of the 1980s), and have eventually professed faith in Christ and joined the overseas Chinese church (especially in the 1990s). However, PRCs remain an enigma to these cross-cultural workers seeking to evangelize and disciple them. Why?

First, PRCs pose an unprecedented challenge because they (like intellectuals coming out of the former Soviet republics) are some of the most avid readers, deep thinkers and passionate debaters in the contemporary international scene. Educated in the "dialectical materialist" method, they want to delve into the bottom of every issue, and explore its many sides. Western and overseas Chinese Christians, educated largely with only the inductive scientific method (and often in its popular, crude form), find themselves ill-equipped to deal with highly educated people who think dialectically. We fail to answer many of their questions, not because we do not have the answers in the Christian faith, but because many of us have yet to begin to understand their mode of thinking.

Second, PRCs (like their Russian and Ukranian counterparts) want to know what Jesus Christ can do for China. How can

Christianity, understood as a historical and sociological-cultural institution, as well as a system of thought expressed through cultural symbols (such as literature, art, music, and schools), contribute to China's economic, educational, social, political, and cultural transformation as China emerges from the 1989 crisis? "Model A" and "Model B" evangelists will have a difficult time walking this journey alongside their mainland Chinese friends. What does Jesus have to say about politics, economics, business ethics, the family, the legal system, rural development, aesthetics, poetic theory, and Chinese and western philosophy? In the words of an international student ministry worker, Chinese intellectuals no longer seek hospitality and compassion; their greatest felt need is reality: how does the Christian faith play out in the real world? What does being "salt and light" mean in a Chinese context?

The challenge today is "Model C" evangelism. We do not wish to neglect the need for a personal presentation of the gospel in its proper time and in ways understood by PRCs, and we hold deep respect for the need to disciple and nurture new believers into maturity. At the same time, "Model C" calls for an examination of their and our worldviews: how do PRCs think, and why? And by extension, how do we, as cross-cultural evangelists, think, and why?

The editors invite you to explore in depth the mindset, the agonies and the cries of contemporary mainland Chinese intellectuals. This book will be a beginning in that search. Read it carefully, prayerfully, and deliberately. Where it makes you cry, stop and pray. Where it puzzles or even disturbs you, stop and reflect: What are some of your own assumptions as you read? And how can we all be more effective "Model C" communicators of the good news of the kingdom of God in Jesus Christ?

Welcome to the world of PRCs — mainland Chinese intellectuals.

# ACKNOWLEDGEMENTS

The co-editors of this volume would like to thank the many colleagues who offered encouragement, advice and help in the process of compiling, editing and publishing this volume. Without their help this project would not have been brought to completion.

Dr. Carol Lee Hamrin (Johns Hopkins University), Dr. Brent Fulton (Wheaton College) and Dr. Tony Carnes (Columbia University) offered much encouragement to publish works about and by Chinese intellectuals for the larger reading public in the West. Dr. Katie Rawson was one of the first authors who contributed articles to the volume. Colleagues at Christian Communications Inc. of Canada were available for consultation in the publishing process. Each author represented in this volume, as well as the copyright holder of the poems in chapter 6, granted permission for reprinting their works, or having them translated. Student assistants put much work into the initial typing, screening, compiling, abstracting, editing and proofreading of the chapters: Sharon Hsu, Jonathan Lee, Yan Li, Brian Sole and Kirk Neuroth at Wheaton College; Jeff Vaughn of Covenant Theological Seminary; and Arthur Lee Hsu at Fuller Theological Seminary. At

China Horizon, Janet Chen scrutinized the manuscript in cooperation with the co-editors, to bring the work to its final stage.

Finally, the co-editors would like to thank our spouses, Mildred Ling and Tom Bieler, for their sacrifices and support, as this manuscript went through its many stages.

We would like to dedicate this volume to the countless, nameless laborers who have reached out to mainland Chinese students and scholars, both in the West and around the world, and have prayed for, encouraged, supported, and discipled these keen minds for the kingdom of God.

# CHINESE INTELLECTUALS AND THE GOSPEL

# A Second Chance

*Samuel Ling*

## A New Millennium and the Search for Modern China

A new millennium is dawning and everything in China seems to be new. A new generation of young people, comparable in mindset to Generations X and Y in the West, searches for material riches and temporal pleasure. New skyscrapers grace the skylines of Shanghai and other cities. Promising to weather the financial crisis in Asia, China's leaders continue to push for economic growth and modernization. As state enterprises are dismantled, the private sector is becoming dominant.

Will the twenty-first century be China's century in the world? If China does become a world leader, will Christian ideas influence her direction? Her goals?

Those who forget history are doomed to repeat it. And China brings a battery of incredible and painful memories into the twenty-first century. The twentieth century began with unprecedented national humiliation with the Boxer Uprising, when China was squarely defeated by the West and Japan in 1900. In 1905, the Confucian civil service examination was abolished, thus eliminating the ladder of success for any young boy growing up in China. By 1911, Sun Yat-sen's young revolutionaries overthrew the Qing dynasty, and a republic was born. But after a brief period of "republican" government (1912-16), the nation was plunged into civil war. Chiang Kai-shek's victory in 1927 merely pacified regional warlords who ruled by force and violence. Refugees began pouring into the cities.

Soon Japan invaded Manchuria (1931) and occupied much of the mainland (1937-45) which Chiang governed from remote Chongqing. At the end of eight years of suffering and retrenchment, the Allies proclaimed victory in 1945. But China continued to suffer through a civil war between the Nationalists and Communists. On October 1, 1949, Mao Zedong declared that "the Chinese people have stood up," and the People's Republic of China was born.

Fifty years of socialism thoroughly transformed the Chinese people on the mainland. Educated in atheism, socialism, and Darwinism, young Chinese intellectuals sought to attain the Maoist ideal of the Socialist Man during the Cultural Revolution (1966-76). However, what began as an experiment for holistic socialist education ended in the most inhumane disaster in Chinese history. Internal power struggles in the Communist Party left China devastated, and a whole generation of young adults disillusioned and largely unemployed.

After Mao died in 1976, the "Gang of Four," including Mao's wife Jiang Qing, was blamed for the horrors of the Cultural Revolution. In 1979, the United States recognized the People's Republic of China. Deng Xiaopeng, a pragmatic leader in post-Mao China, was determined to move ahead with his Four Modernizations to bring 1.2 billion people into the twentieth century. His efforts have been continued by Jiang Zemin since 1997.

Meanwhile the Republic of China in Taiwan has transformed into a modern, industrialized economy and a democratic society with direct elections. Hong Kong, the largest container port in the world and a major global financial center, was returned to Chinese rule in 1997. Overseas Chinese in Asia and North America are using their diligence, endurance, and skills to establish vibrant communities in Southeast Asia, North America, Europe, and elsewhere. According to Tu Wei-ming, the New Confucian philosopher who has taught at Harvard and the East-West Center in Honolulu, the margin (overseas Chinese) will once again lead the center (the mainland).

In the 1980s China searched for new ideas to guide her Four Modernizations. Intellectuals looked to the West for guidance and encouragement. A decade of exploration resulted in the student movement at Tiananmen Square in the Spring of 1989. The June Fourth tragedy symbolized a "dead end." Once again, China had to start all over to search for a guiding light as she sought to modernize.

What ideas will truly guide the "search for modern China?" Will China be an anti-foreign, militant, and nationalistic people in the twentieth century? Will nihilism, materialism, and atheism be the governing ideas for the worldview of the Chinese people? Will Buddhism and folk religions rise again to dominate their thinking? Will a new version of Confucianism find a hearing among China's students and teachers? What is the place of the Christian gospel, the worldview based on the Old and New Testaments, in China's search for an all-comprehensive national ideology?

## A Battlefield of Ideas: Christianity and the May Fourth Movement (1915-1927)

The Christian gospel was a contestant in China's battle of the mind earlier in the twentieth century. Soon after Sun Yat-sen's revolution of 1911, key Chinese intellectuals realized that a

3

constitution and a parliament were insufficient to transform China into a modern, strong, and prosperous state. Something more fundamental was at stake: China needed a new culture, a new set of ideas, and values to guide individual and social behavior. The "New Culture Movement" was born.

The most influential magazine read by young people during this "May Fourth Period" (1915-1927) was called *New Youth*, edited by the journalist and activist Chen Duxiu. Launched in the Fall of 1915, Chen called for the emancipation of the individual, free thought, and experimentation. He invited a society conducive to the promotion of democracy and science, the abolition of all Confucianist and feudal ideas and institutions, and a vision for the future based on the Social Darwinism of Thomas Huxley and Herbert Spencer. In short, all things ancient and Chinese must go; all things modern and western were to be implemented.

The May Fourth demonstrations in 1919 taught China's students the magical power of mass rallies and political organization. Into a climate of anti-foreign, anti-imperialistic anger, Marxist ideas entered through Soviet agents and an indigenous Marxism study group which met at the librarian's office in Beijing University. Mao Zedong, an assistant to librarian Li Dazhao, was a junior member of the group. The Chinese Communist Party was organized as an underground movement in July 1921.

As young Chinese Communists sought to influence their contemporaries with their worldview and program for change, the battlefield of ideas began to take a significant turn. Communists claimed that Christianity was unscientific and was a tool of imperialism. Religion was an impediment to social progress. Communist students led the first Anti-Christian Movement in 1922, as well as the second wave of anti-Christian fermentation from 1924 to 1925. Western Christian missionaries, as well as Protestant Chinese leaders, were caught on the defensive. How should Christian churches and institutions in China change to meet these challenges? Could one be a Christian and a patriotic Chinese at the same time?

Liberal Protestants in China, both Western and Chinese, began to demonstrate that Christianity was compatible with Confucianism, at a time when intellectuals called for the total abolition of Confucianist ideas! They also explained that Christianity could be a significant instrument to foster a spirit of democracy to produce Chinese leaders, and to bring about a society based on equality and freedom. The kingdom of God was to arrive on the good earth of China through liberal education and gradual change. The Sermon on the Mount was to guide China's transformation. Little was said about Adam's sin and the fall of humanity, the atoning death of Christ on the cross, or salvation by God's grace in Christ.

The May Fourth search for China's ideology came to a close in 1927 as civil war ended. Chiang Kai-shek ordered all students to return to their books in 1928. China entered a period of conservatism, and the nineteenth century scholar-warlord, Zeng Guofan, was hailed as a hero for junior and senior high youth. The Communists fled to the countryside, and were later forced to go on "The Long March" in 1935 and resettle in Yanan. All seemed quiet on the battlefield of ideas.

Evangelical preachers like John Sung, Wang Mingdao, Watchman Nee, Calvin Chao, and Andrew Gih began their revivalist careers shortly after 1925. From 1927 to 1949, many high school and university students turned to Christ and dedicated their lives to evangelism. Little did they realize that they were preparing themselves for a period of suffering and persecution

(1949-1976). With great fervor, Sung, Wang, and Nee exhorted young and old alike to separate themselves from the world and live holy lives for Jesus Christ. A biblical, Christian worldview, which called Christians to transform the world, but not be transformed by it, was rarely presented.

## A Second Chance

PRC students emerged from the Cultural Revolution (1966-1976) as some of the most well read intellectuals in the late twentieth century. Like their counterparts in Russia and the former Soviet republics, Chinese students are trained to think, write, debate, and handle profound issues in literature, the arts, philosophy, the social sciences, and politics.

On June 4, 1989, Christians outside China (Chinese or otherwise), were glued to their television sets, shedding tears of support for the student demonstrators overrun by the Chinese Liberation Army. Chinese evangelical leaders took to the streets in Hong Kong and Los Angeles, calling on God to judge with justice. Soon China returned to an awkward normality. Christian professionals and English teachers returned to China. The economy took off in China and in the United States, as China became a major trading partner with the United States. The Communist Party's desperate struggle to respond to unprecedented changes after 1989 and to continue to govern 1.2 billion people, made its position very vulnerable; so it harassed and persecuted Christians who might destabilize the nation, just like what had been done in Eastern Europe. Many intellectuals, working for business enterprises rather than reading and writing philosophy, found that "to get rich is glorious."

Post-1989 China shares one thing in common with post-1919 China. Despite the economic changes, China still needs to find an all-comprehensive ideology or worldview to guide her into the future. Since Christian liberal theology lost the distinctiveness of Christ and fundamentalism withdrew from engaging the culture, both proved to be inadequate. What can the church offer China? As Chinese students meet Christian teachers in English classes in China, or international student workers on campuses in the West, they want to know: What does Jesus Christ have to say to China's political, economic, cultural, educational, and family needs? Will Christianity offer a viable voice to shape China's future?

Post-Tiananmen Square China can be compared with two other periods in Western history. During the sixteenth century, Martin Luther and John Calvin preached the gospel of salvation by grace through faith to Europeans enslaved by medieval Catholic legalism and authoritarianism. The gospel of Jesus Christ is all about grace: a Father in heaven, loving, accepting, and transforming his children as they come to Him in faith. China today needs to hear the strong word of grace!

Then, in the eighteenth century, after Luther and Calvin's influence began to wane as a secular, commercialized society took shape in England and America, the Great Awakening called Christians back to repentance and a disciplined lifestyle committed to the glory of God and the transformation of society. Jonathan Edwards both witnessed the movement of repentance in New England and sought to shape and sustain it. Responding to the church's skeptical critics during the Enlightenment period, Edwards interpreted the experiences of the Christian soul, both in the light of the Bible, and in response to eighteenth century skepticism. A biblical worldview made a significant contribution in shaping the new republic, balancing and tempering the secular, Deist ideas of the time as America adopted her Constitution in 1789.

7

Compare this experience with France. France endured mob rule during the 1789 Revolution, followed by Napoleon's dictatorship. Why the difference? In large measure, Reformation ideas embodied in the Great Awakening tempered the American experiment in modern democracy.

Evangelical outreach to Chinese intellectuals today needs to be similarly undergirded with a philosophy of history grounded in the Bible. Evangelistic fervor and fidelity to the gospel of the cross of Jesus Christ need to be complemented with intellectual rigor and integrity. As the late Francis Schaeffer called upon Christians in the 1970s to provide "honest answers to honest questions," so twenty-first century evangelicals must be prepared and equipped with a biblical, compassionate, and relevant apologetic.

What Christian ideas can guide China? What does the Bible have to say about constitutional democracy, economic progress, business ethics, divorce and remarriage, and postmodern art and literary criticism - not to mention the challenge of New Confucianism and folk religion in China?

This is the church's second chance to bring hope to China, by presenting a Christian worldview to her leaders. Let us not miss it. Again.

# The Gospel and Culture in Chinese History

*Jonathan Chao*

The historical interaction between the gospel and Chinese culture reveals several key factors leading to the success or failure of the gospel to penetrate Chinese thought and society.

1. What was the nature of the dominant Chinese culture?

2. What was the political ideology of the governing authority?

3. What kind of message did the missionaries or preachers try to communicate to the Chinese?

4. How did the missionaries view the Chinese people and their culture? How did their attitude influence their mission work, especially their methods?

5. How receptive were the Chinese people to the Christian message? If they resisted, why did they resist, and what was the nature of their resistance?

6. How did the Chinese perceive the gospel bearer and the Christian message at that particular period? What influenced their perception?

7. How did Christians or missionaries seek to overcome Chinese resistance to the gospel? To what extent were they successful, and to what extent did they fail?

When seen in light of these questions, it becomes obvious that the interaction has been quite complicated. However, I will try to summarize some of the more salient features related to the gospel and Chinese culture in order to give insight for those who are presenting the gospel to the Chinese people today.

## The Gospel and Chinese Culture in Historical Context

In general, church historians speak of four entries of the Christian faith into China. They are: (1) the entry of the Nestorians during the Tang Dynasty (618-907); (2) the return of the Nestorians and the entry of Catholic missionaries during the Yuan Dynasty (1279-1368); (3) the entry of the Jesuits during the Ming Dynasty (1368-1644); and (4) the entry of Protestant and Catholic missionaries following the first Opium War (1839-1842). Our historical reflections will be based on the pre-1949 period.

### *Nestorian Christianity during the Tang Dynasty*

Nestorian missionaries came to China in A.D.635 They represented the Antiochene branch of early Christianity with strong emphasis on the humanity of Jesus, a view not generally accepted by evangelicals today. Changan, the capital of the Tang Dynasty, was then a cosmopolitan and pluralistic city. Daoism had a strong hold among the Confucian literati. Buddhism had adjusted itself to Chinese traditions and developed its beliefs in response to the needs of the Chinese society (317-589), and was enjoying independent growth as a Chinese faith.

Nestorian Christianity was well received by the Tang court. It bestowed its imperial favor upon the missionaries by granting them the privilege of translating their Scriptures at the imperial library and by providing financial subsidy for their work. The

Nestorian missionaries honored the Tang emperors by painting their images on church walls. With such imperial favor Nestorianism grew and monasteries were erected in many cities.

However, the Nestorians had a hard time communicating the Christian message to the Chinese people. In translating their Scriptures into Chinese, or in expounding their doctrines, they felt compelled to use Buddhist and Daoist terms to make them understandable.

The Nestorians did not seem to have developed a critical method of apologetics. Thus, after a hundred years of adapting their message to Buddhist and Daoist concepts and terms, they gradually lost their Christian distinctive. This difference can be clearly seen in the documents produced before 720 and those produced after; this is especially evident in a monument erected in 781.

As the Confucianists grew in power within the Tang court, they began suppressing Buddhism, culminating in the persecution of 845 Nestorian Christianity was also wiped out during that time.

Why did Nestorian Christianity fail to survive the persecution?

First of all, Buddhism and Daoism had a much more sophisticated system of philosophical and religious thought than Nestorian Christianity. The latter did not develop a strong theological base from which they could critically understand the complexity of Chinese culture. Out of the necessity for communication, they adapted their teaching to Buddhist and Daoist concepts; in the process they lost the uniqueness, and hence the transforming power, of the gospel. Their mistake was uncritical adaptation.

Secondly, the Nestorians failed to develop a school of theology where Chinese converts could be trained in biblical and

11

theological scholarship, and where an indigenous clergy could be trained.

Lastly, the Nestorians' witness depended on imperial favor, and when political hostility and persecution grew they vanished.

## Nestorians and Catholics during the Yuan Dynasty

In Sung China (960-1279) Buddhism and Daoism further interacted with, and exerted considerable influence on Confucianism, producing what was later known as Neo-Confucianism. Chinese political, social, and cultural institutions reached the peak of their development, with Confucianism dominating Chinese thought and institutions overall.

When the Mongols conquered the Sung and established the Yuan Dynasty (1279-1368), Chinese (Han) rule was replaced by foreign rule. Consequently, Confucian orthodoxy was temporarily suspended, and foreign ideas and religions were allowed to flourish again in a pluralistic society. The Nestorians returned to China and established themselves in fifteen cities, with a bishop in Xian, the capital. By 1300, Nestorians numbered thirty thousand in China. The Nestorians served as scribes in the Yuan court and also engaged in commerce. The Franciscans also arrived from Europe. In 1305 Father John of Montecorvino (1247-1328) was reported to have baptized six thousand Chinese converts.

But when the Han Chinese overthrew the Mongol dynasty, the policy of toleration of foreign religions ceased. During the new Ming Dynasty (1368-1644), both Nestorian and Catholic churches disappeared.

Two factors appeared to have contributed to the disappearance of the Nestorians and the Catholics at the beginning of the Ming Dynasty. The first seems to be their failure to produce a large number of converts who were theologically strong and culturally learned to survive the drastic political and social changes. The second factor lies in the anti-foreign, closed-door policy of the Confucian Ming state.

## Catholic Missions During the Late-Ming and Early Qing Dynasty

When the Jesuit Francis Xavier first reached Macao in 1552, Ming China was closed to foreign contacts. The Ming state, then ruled by its Confucian official literati, was conservative, Sino-centric, and self-complacent. It resisted the entry of foreign missionaries. All evangelistic attempts by the Jesuits prior to Matteo Ricci (1552-1610) had failed. It was only due to Ricci's patience, indigenous scholarship, and cultural adaptability that Catholic Christianity finally gained a re-entry into China. It took him eighteen years to move from Guangzhou (Canton) to Beijing (1582-1600). Ricci, a well-trained Jesuit, not only learned the Chinese language well, but also became an expert in Chinese culture. He sought to understand the Chinese people, and befriended Chinese scholars and officials. Because of his discreet approach and adaptability, Catholicism flourished in China for nearly a hundred years.

Ricci adopted a method of accommodation to Chinese culture. He would permit Chinese converts to venerate or worship their ancestors and to keep their Chinese customs. He also offered his Western learning as a service to the Ming court, which eventually employed his successors to head up the board of astronomy.

However, Ricci's method of accommodation was challenged by subsequent arrivals of Franciscans and Dominicans who interpreted ancestral worship as idolatry and who appealed to the

Pope for correction. The Pope officially prohibited Chinese Catholics to participate in ancestral worship. This action infuriated the Kangxi Emperor (1662-1723), who eventually expelled all Catholic missionaries except for a few Jesuit astronomers. After 1724 Chinese Catholics were persecuted for over a hundred years. It was not until the issuing of the Edict of Toleration in 1846 that Chinese Catholics had their guilty status removed, and it was not until the Treaty of Tianjin (1858) and the Convention of Beijing (1860) that foreign missionaries and Chinese Christians were allowed to preach and practice the Christian faith in China.

What historical lessons can we learn from the Jesuit experience in China? If the inter-mission struggle over the Rites Controversy had not occurred, the Kangxi Emperor, who had already developed an open attitude toward the Catholics, might have believed in Christianity, and become the second Constantine, the Emperor of Rome, who ended the persecution of Christians in 313 A.D.

The Catholic failure during this period was probably not a failure of the Jesuits to understand theology, but of the Franciscans and Dominicans to understand Chinese culture, as well as a joint failure of both to see the unity of the Christian faith. The Qing court was not unreceptive to the new foreign faith, but it was not tolerant of an alien authority dictating the beliefs of its subjects. It was not a religious resistance, but a political one. The Jesuit experience reveals a very important fact: in China resistance to the gospel was not so much cultural as it was political. Conversely, receptivity is conditioned more by political considerations than by cultural factors.

## Christian Missions in the Modern Era

The fourth entry of Christianity into China took place within the larger context of Western commercial and colonial expansion in the nineteenth century. Protestant and Catholic missionaries followed in the steps of their governments' colonial expansion and took advantage of their governments' military victories. Missionaries first gained a foothold in the five ports (Guangzhou, Xiamen, Fuzhou, Ningbo, and Shanghai) which China was forced to open to foreign trade when it lost the first Opium War (1839-1842). They gained the right to travel and to propagate the Christian faith through the Treaties of Tianjin and Beijing. This manner of gaining an entry into China differed from all previous entries, and brought much resistance to the gospel on the part of both the people and the government in subsequent years.

While the nature of Chinese culture remained similar from the Tang to the late Qing Dynasty, the political identity of the gospel bearer changed drastically. The Chinese people and the official-gentry class did not perceive missionaries as propagators of religious faith, but as foreigners who defeated them in war and as cultural aggressors who sought to impose cultural change on them. Many missionaries in the nineteenth century had a "messianic complex," firmly believing in the superiority of Western culture, and openly despising Chinese culture as decadent and dehumanizing. They regarded the destruction of Chinese culture as one of their chief tasks, and through mission schools, they desired to create a new kind of Christian Chinaman.

The situation that developed was one of alienation and hostility between the missionaries and the Chinese people. The mainstream of the Chinese society, especially the official-gentry class, opposed Christianity. Only the poor and the marginal people believed in order to receive personal help or material gains. The history of modern missions in China was filled with incidents of conflict between the missionaries and their converts on the one hand, and Chinese local leaders on the other. This culminated in the tragedy of the Boxer Rebellion in 1900, in which over two hundred missionaries and more than two thousands Chinese converts died.

The late Qing Dynasty represented the worst situation in the relationship between the gospel and Chinese culture. First of all, the gunboat diplomacy of the Western powers and the missionaries' uncritical identification with it totally discredited them as gospel bearers. Secondly, the missionaries' negative attitude toward Chinese culture prevented them from seeking to understand the complexities of Chinese culture, and this led them to develop an anti-Chinese cultural syndrome. Lastly, the Chinese people were alienated from the missionaries and the church, so that the gospel could not be considered on its own merit. Again, the gospel was rejected not on cultural grounds, but on political grounds.

With the collapse of the Qing Dynasty and the establishment of the republic by Sun Yat-sen's revolutionaries (1911), the relationship between the gospel and the Chinese people enhanced. This improvement came from a subsequent change in political institutions, and from the termination of the Confucian state orthodoxy. The new republic established a constitutional government and adopted the Western principle of separation of church and state. Chinese Christians could, for the first time in centuries, enjoy full legal status. Ideologically, the government was not committed to any official orthodoxy, and thus a state of ideological pluralism prevailed. Under such a change, mission work in China flourished, and independent Chinese churches began to grow.

However, during the May Fourth Period (1919-1927), modern Chinese intellectuals developed a new anti-religious and anti-Christian attitude which weighed against Chinese reception of the gospel. A series of political and cultural developments evolved during those few years. First of all, Western international injustice in the Peace Treaty at Versailles triggered a wave of student patriotism. The May Fourth Period set the stage for modern Chinese anti-foreignism, and awakened the Chinese intellectuals to search for a new cultural alternative to the Confucian tradition, so as to create a new China. The New Culture Movement was to be based on science and reason, and borrowed a new form of anti-religious thinking from the West. The rise of the Chinese Communist movement in 1921 and the reorganization of the Guomindang (Sun Yat-sen's Nationalist Party) ushered in a brief period of collaboration between the Chinese Communist Party and the Nationalist Party. A new wave of anti-Christian propaganda was part of their joint anti-imperialist campaign (1926-1927).

Therefore foreign missionaries and Chinese Christians were confronted with a new hostile cultural situation. The New Culture Movement was anti-religious in character, and the anti-imperialist movement was anti-Christian in particular. These movements created an ugly image of Christianity as unscientific, a hindrance to social progress, and a tool of imperialist cultural aggression. Such propaganda became the truth in the minds of Chinese youths in that period. As the messengers were thus discredited, the message could not be heard. During the period of the Nationalist-Communist collaboration (1924-1927), advocates of anti-imperialism sought to develop a new official orthodoxy in the form of Marxist-Leninist ideology, which sought to expel all other competing ideologies.

Chinese Christians, intellectuals, and church leaders, especially those in the liberal camp, tried to overcome this new resistance to the gospel by adapting the gospel to the scientific demands of the New Culture Movement. As a result, they openly rejected the essentials of the gospel: the virgin birth and the death and resurrection of Jesus Christ. The conservatives did not have many spokesmen to respond. In response to anti-imperialist pressures, Protestant church leaders separated themselves from foreign missions (symbols of imperialism) and developed independent and indigenous Chinese churches, which identified with the aspirations of the Chinese people and was integrated with Chinese culture.

This attempt at integration proceeded along five approaches. The first adapted external forms of expression from Chinese tradition. The second injected Christianity into Chinese culture in an attempt to Christianize it. The third planted the seed of Christianity into the soil of Chinese culture. The fourth sought common ground between Christian and Chinese ethics. And the fifth synchronized elements of Christianity with the best of Western and Chinese culture.

The response of the church to the New Culture Movement and the anti-Christian campaigns in the 1920s represented a Chinese Christian response rather than one by foreign missionaries. Since Chinese Christians shared a common cultural and national identity with their fellow Chinese critics, their attitude toward Chinese culture differed from that of their missionary predecessors. Theirs was not an attitude of spite, but one of solidarity. As Christians they had received something from outside their Chinese tradition, and the challenge they faced was how to integrate their Christian faith with Chinese culture. The outcome of their attempts at integration was less than satisfactory, because their understanding of the gospel was inadequate, having been nurtured in the Western liberal Christian tradition.

After the Nationalist Party and the Communists split in 1927, the anti-Christian movement came to an end. The Nanjing government of Chiang Kai-shek became anti-Communist, and adopted a pluralistic acceptance of non-Communist ideologies. The pattern of separation of church and state, which had characterized the early republican period (1912-1915), was resumed, and Christianity was once again tolerated. But the character of modern pluralistic Chinese culture was still very much an extension of the New Culture thinking, and hence anti-religious in outlook. The negative effects of the New Culture Movement and the Anti-Christian Movement can still be felt among the Chinese people today, particularly among the intellectuals in the universities in China, Taiwan, and Hong Kong.

After 1949, the pluralistic character of modern Chinese culture on the mainland was forcibly changed to a monolithic socialist culture of the Marxist-Leninist and Maoist model. Marxism became the dominating official orthodoxy. Christianity, along with other religions, was tolerated as long as it was under state control. The nature of Chinese social political culture and how Chinese Christians sought to respond to it have been the subject of much attention and concern among Christians outside China. Enduring suffering and persecution, the church in China grew in both size and influence. Meanwhile, the nature of Chinese culture had been transformed, through the dispersion of the Chinese people, into a complex mosaic. Chinese people are found in Taiwan, Hong Kong, Southeast Asia, the West, and all over the world. Some of the more important components of modern Chinese culture include legacies from Confucianism, Buddhism, Daoism, rationalism, scientism (a blind belief in the almighty power of science), evolution, Marxism-Leninism and Mao Zedong thought, as well as contemporary capitalism, consumerism, and nihilism. At the level of the masses, there is also a variety of religious beliefs and practice mixing Buddhism with folk religions and superstitions. Communicators of the gospel today must realize that the Chinese mind is complex, and that the Chinese people live in a complex cultural context in a process of rapid change.

## The Gospel and Chinese Culture: An Analysis from History

The encounter of Christianity with culture in the context of Chinese history is summarized in the chart at the end of the chapter. From this history we can make some general observations:

First of all, political, rather than cultural factors, govern the receptivity of the Chinese people to the gospel. The attitude of the Chinese state toward gospel bearers is a strong factor influencing the extent of the people's receptivity to the gospel. It is therefore important to understand how the gospel bearer is viewed by those in power at any moment in history.

Secondly, whenever the Chinese state was dominated by Sino-centric, Confucian literati, the latter would use political power to promote a Confucian state orthodoxy, and to control other ideas and religions. This was true during the Tang, Ming and Qing Dynasties. Marxist-Maoist orthodoxy has produced similar, if not stricter, state control of other ideologies and religions. This being the case, we ought to pray toward the emergence of a pluralistic culture where the government supports no official orthodoxy.

Thirdly, the gospel bearer should have a favorable attitude towards the dominant culture, especially that advocated by the state, in order for the gospel to be received. Confrontation in the Chinese context has proven to be rather disastrous. More friendly approaches to Chinese culture need to be explored.

Lastly, the history of Christian encounters with Chinese culture and political power reveals the following basic approaches:

1. *Independent evangelistic work* under a situation of religious freedom - such as that of the Nestorians and Catholics during the Yuan Dynasty, and that of Protestant missions and Chinese Christians during the early republican era after 1911. In such situations, the messengers of the gospel were not forced to reckon with Chinese cultural factors. They presented Christianity to the Chinese people as one of many competing ideologies.

2. *Accommodation* was used by both the Jesuits in the Ming Dynasty and some missionaries in the nineteenth century. Here the missionaries made concessions to Chinese cultural demands for the sake of immediate receptivity, without necessarily committing to doctrinal syncretism.

3. *Adaptation* was used by the Nestorians, the liberal Protestants during the New Culture Movement (1919-1927), and by the Three-Self Patriotic Movement in contemporary China (1949-present). Adaptation involves doctrinal change on the part of the gospel, in order to be received by a dominant culture. Adaptation of the gospel content usually leads to some kind of transmutation of the gospel, so that its distinctive doctrines of salvation are lost, and Christian evangelism became ineffective.

4. *Transformation* was practiced by Protestant missionaries in the late nineteenth century as well as during the republican era (1928-1949). The House Church movement in China today also adopts the approach of transformation. Transformation seeks to change Chinese culture into some kind of Christian culture, through a long process of evangelism, education, and social reconstruction.

Today the church is vibrant on Chinese soil, as well as among the Chinese diaspora around the world. Having learned lessons from the past, how will the church continue to develop appropriate and effective evangelistic approaches in this complex, changing context?

## The Gospel and Chinese Culture in Historical Perspective

| Period | Messengers | Nature of Culture | Political Ideology | Approach Developed | Receptivity to the Gospel | Attitude Towards Dominant Culture |
|---|---|---|---|---|---|---|
| Tang | Nestorian missionaries | Daoism, Buddhism, Confucianism | Ideological Pluralism, Confucianism | Adaptation | Received imperial favor, later rejection | Respect Conciliatory |
| Yuan | Nestorian & Catholic missionaries | Pluralistic Culture | Foreign rule; no official orthodoxy | Independent Development | Received by foreigners & some Chinese | Co-existence |
| Ming | Jesuits | Confucian Dominance | Confucian Orthodoxy | Accommodation | Receptive by Ching Court | Appreciation |
| | Dominicans & Franciscans | Confucian Dominance | Confucian Orthodoxy | Confrontation | Rejection by the Court | Reservation |
| Qing (1842-1911) | British, American & European missionaries | Confucian Dominance plus Others | Confucian Orthodoxy | Accommodation, Confrontation, & Transformation | Rejection by literati | Despise |
| Early Republic (1912-1919) | Foreign missionaries & Chinese Christians | Pluralistic: traditional Chinese & Western | Separation of Church & State | Independent Development | Very Receptive | Mutual Tolerance |
| May Fourth Era (1919-1927) | Chinese Christians | Rise of scientific & rationalistic new culture in the midst of Confucian culture | Rise of Rationalistic Marxist Orthodoxy | Adaptation & Integration | Rejection | Indentification & Conciliatory |
| Late Republic (1928-1949) | Chinese Christians | Pluralistic | Strong no official orthodoxy except "Sanminism" separation of Church & State | Independent Development | Normal Receptivity | Indentification |
| The PRC (1949-1985) | Chinese Church Leaders (TSPM) | Marxism, Leninism & Maoism | Marxist official orthodoxy | Adaptation | Avoidance & limited reception | Identification |
| | Chinese believer (House Church) | Marxism, Leninism & Maoism | Marxist official orthodoxy | Confrontation, Transformation | Very Receptive | Rejection or Accommodation |

# Contemporary Chinese Intellectuals, I: Thought Reform and Revolution, 1949-1979

*Stacey Bieler*

Today's Chinese intellectuals, a significant group both needed and feared by the leaders of China, follow an ancient model established by Confucian scholars. For two thousand years their predecessors, the literati, were pulled by their loyalty to the ruler and by their obligation to speak out when the government deviated from benevolence towards the people. Although the literati had always been a small number, they influenced the country's decision-making process. They did not criticize as a group because the leaders would regard them as subversive. They used indirect language because the appearance of consensus was necessary to preserve the legitimacy of a Chinese regime. Their methods included essays, philosophical debate, historical interpretation, literary criticism, poetry, and drama.[1] The literati sometimes risked punishment or death for offering criticisms. Though many failed to live up to their call, others were revered as heroes who displayed integrity of character. Today's intellectuals live with the knowledge of this past model.

Since 1949 the cycles of relaxation and repression toward intellectuals have been rooted in an inherent tension between government leaders and intellectuals. The total loyalty and unquestioning discipline required of party members by Leninist theory makes today's intellectuals face the dilemma: "How to serve their country and help make it rich, powerful and modern without compromising their intellectual and moral values."[2] The government's ambivalence towards the influence of intellectuals causes cycles of "cold winds" coming from top leadership (when intellectuals need to be careful about expressing their views) or "warm winds" (when they are freer to express their views). Campaigns often began by focusing on one person whose complaint had "crossed the line" deemed unacceptable in the government's eyes. Chinese proverbs illustrate this pattern: "pointing to the mulberry to revile the ash" or "killing the rooster to warn the monkey." After the pattern of regular campaigns became established, most intellectuals became self-regulating in order not to get caught crossing an ever-shifting line. One intellectual wrote that there had been forty campaigns in the first forty years in the People's Republic of China.

## Campaigns against Returned Students, 1949-1955

The People's Republic of China was established on October 1, 1949. The new leaders had to rebuild China's social fabric after years of chaos: the fall of the Qing Dynasty in 1911, disruption by warlords from 1916-1928, the war with Japan from 1937-1945, and a bloody civil war from 1945-1949.

The government used various examples to tell intellectuals what limits of complaints the new government would put up with. A movie released in December 1950, which was at first praised, was denounced several months later as "propaganda for a feudal culture." A writer who asked for freedom on subject matter and artistic form was denounced as a counter-revolutionary, stripped of his official post and finally jailed.[3] Then in 1951-1952 and 1954-1955, the government held campaigns against Hu Shih, a 1917 graduate of

26

Columbia University, and formerly a professor at Beijing University, who had advocated American liberalism. He was then living in the United States.[4]

The government needed the intellectuals to build the new country, but intellectuals, especially those who had been trained overseas, were seen as tainted with undesirable qualities such as elitism, individualism, admiration of the United States, and preference for Western curriculum.[5] For seven years, intellectuals went through thought reform: debates, study groups, political classes, writing autobiographies and forced confessions. For weeks and months, intellectuals would be kept in suspense about their future, until they became nervous wrecks or "a rebirth or a new sense" of values dawned upon them.[6]

## "Let A Hundred Flowers Bloom," 1956

After seven years, the leaders of China thought that national reconstruction had been a success. It was time to allow the intellectuals some freedom to express themselves, hoping that they would comment about the progress the government had made. In order to encourage the intellectuals to speak, a famous proverb was announced: "Let a hundred flowers blossom and let a hundred schools contend." Mao Zedong hoped for well-intentioned criticism to be expressed "as gentle as a breeze or a mild rain."[7]

Instead, Mao received a flood of criticism and "poisonous weeds" rather than flowers came out into the open. The intellectuals complained about the lack of academic freedom and the interference of uneducated party cadres who had gotten positions due to political reasons or nepotism. They even directed attacks against Communist ideology and the top leadership. Most alarming was the violent complaints by the students who were the benefactors of the new republic and were the future of the country.[8] The intellectuals had "bloomed," not realizing that a cold wind was coming.

## The Anti-Rightist Campaign, 1956-1957

So shocked were they by the intellectuals' response that the government took two months to respond. The leaders saw that the intellectuals had only been playing a charade with their self-criticisms and confessions; they had not really changed their hearts. Their independent spirits continued to remain strong.[9]

The government launched the Anti-Rightist Campaign against the "poisonous weeds" who had come out into the open. General Secretary Deng Xiaoping was in charge of the campaign. Public hearings were staged and student leaders were executed. Intellectuals were sent to work in villages and into Northwest China to be reeducated. Research institutions became production units.[10] One professor, in objection, wrote to Mao and said, "We have applied to intellectuals methods of punishment which peasants would not apply to landlords and workers would not apply to capitalists."[11] He told how intellectuals had committed suicide rather than face persecution.

The label as a "rightist" stuck with people for the next twenty years since everyone in China had a file. This label was used to "round up the usual suspects." Family members were encouraged to break with those whose labels always kept them under suspicion. Rightists also had difficulty advancing in their jobs and receiving housing.

## The Great Leap Forward, 1958-1966

Though China used the Russian language and curriculum in their educational system and sent its students to the Soviet Union to study, it competed with the Soviet Union for pre-eminence of the Communist-controlled countries. Mao wanted China to look better than the Soviet Union by speeding up the process of communizing China. Provincial leaders competed with each other to show how great their agricultural production was. They misled the government by telling about incredible harvests and they sent grain to cities while the peasants in their provinces starved. A former village resident, who came as a graduate student to the United States, recounted how many villagers died of hunger or from eating dirt or bark off trees. The Great Leap Forward caused an economic catastrophe and widespread famine.

After three years some of the Party bureaucrats became disillusioned with Mao's policies. The Party was so desperate that they turned to the intellectuals to revive the economy. Some intellectuals who had been labeled as "rightists" were reinstated. Intellectuals began to criticize Mao and assert their own opinions since they were protected by certain members in the Party leadership. These "patron-client" relations allowed intellectuals to denounce Mao for years without retribution. In retaliation, Mao, who wanted to regain control by "cleaning out" the Party, launched several "rectification campaigns" in 1963 and 1964, but they were superficial and did not get rid of his enemies. In 1964 Mao began talking about the coming of a real campaign.[12]

## The Great Proletarian Cultural Revolution, 1966-1976

Mao launched the Great Proletarian Cultural Revolution in 1966 because of his lack of trust towards the intellectuals. He saw them as competitors since they had influence in the country as "teachers (who instruct the young, i.e., the heirs to the future), scientists (who are responsible for the technical development of the state), and artists and writers (who influence the masses)."[13] In comparison, Mao saw peasants and workers as being pure. He emphasized the political or class background of people; that is, being "red" or revolutionary was better than being an "expert," (one with learning).

The Cultural Revolution officially began with an attack on one historian who wrote a historical play. Then editors of two party newspapers and one party magazine were ousted. People attacked their personal enemies in the name of Mao. With those "patrons" deposed, "clients" lost their protection and were purged. The reign of terror engulfed China's professors, university presidents, editors, journalists, musicians, actors, film directors, writers, and critics.

The Red Guards, a group made up of teenagers, turned against their teachers by beating them, stealing, and burning their books and treasures. They interfered with the highest levels of science and technology, including nuclear weapons research. Schools and universities were closed and scientific work stagnated. Scientists became isolated from the world's scientific developments. Intellectuals and their children were "sent down" to the countryside to learn from the peasants. One of my friends, who is an economist, drove a tractor for several years. Another friend worked in a tea plantation while still another pushed a rice thrasher with her feet all day (the hardest job on the commune). When factions within the Red Guards began fighting against one another in the streets in order to show how patriotic they were, Mao tried to re-open the schools in order to stop civil war. After worker-peasant-soldier teams failed to calm down the schools, Mao sent the Guards to the countryside.

The worst was over by 1970, though on a smaller scale Mao's wife, Jiang Qing, kept the reign of terror going against those in cultural spheres. This lasted until Mao's death in 1976. The government sought to channel the hostilities produced in the Cultural Revolution onto the Gang of Four, which included Mao's wife and three other officials, who were arrested in 1976.[14] As part of a joke, when some talked about the Gang of Four, they would hold up five fingers. Who was the fifth? Mao. But how can you accuse the Father of the Country for being responsible for a national disaster? Many people are still unwilling to admit to what they did as Red Guards. They will say, "I was a Red Guard, but I didn't do anything," but this denial of responsibility means that they have been unable to be forgiven and reconciled.

## The Deng "Dynasty" Begins, 1978-1979

Deng Xiaoping gained control over the Party on December 1978. He had become a Communist while working and studying in France in the 1920s. He was both an old revolutionary, who had been on the Long March and fought with the Eighth Route Army, and a pragmatic modernizer, which had gotten him in trouble with Mao in the past. A joke circulated that Jesus was raised from the dead one time, whereas Deng had been raised three times after being ousted! [The third time was after the 1976 Tiananmen Square demonstrations in memory of Zhou Enlai, the Gang of Four blamed Deng and stripped him of all his posts.]

In 1977 the university entrance examinations were reinstated and some children of intellectuals escaped the countryside and made it into a university. But many felt guilty since their smarter brother, sister, or friend were left behind in rural areas. China began sending scholars, and later students, abroad to study in order to make up for the "ten lost years." Deng began to "rehabilitate" intellectuals by removing their "rightist" labels, often posthumously for the sake of the families. (He was the one who had overseen the labeling twenty years before.)

Since the ability of intellectuals to be heard publicly is dependent upon the tolerance of their political patrons, the diverging interests of the patrons themselves, and factional struggle within the top leadership, their opportunities to influence policy and to suggest programs are always short-lived.

## Notes

[1] Merle Goldman, *China's Intellectuals: Advise and Dissent* (Cambridge, MA: Harvard University Press, 1981), 1, 4, 6.

[2] Merle Goldman and Timothy Cheek, "Introduction," in *Chinese Intellectuals and the State*, eds. Merle Goldman, Timothy Cheek, and Carol Hamrin (Cambridge, MA: Harvard University Press, 1987), 2,3,20.

[3] Adrian Hsia, *The Chinese Cultural Revolution* (London: Orbach and Chambers, 1972), 82, 85.

[4] Jerome B. Grieder, *Hu Shih and the Chinese Renaissance* (Cambridge, MA: Harvard University Press, 1970), 361-363.

[5] Hsia, 79-80.

[6] Vincent Y.C. Shih, "The State of the Intellectuals," in *Communist China, 1949-1969, A Twenty-year Appraisal*, ed. Frank Trager and William Henderson (New York: New York University Press, 1970), 224-225.

[7] Roderick MacFarquhar, *The Hundred Flowers Campaign and The Chinese Intellectuals* (New York: Farrar, Straus and Giroux, 1974), 3.

[8] Hsia, 88. MacFarquhar, 12. See also Jurgen Domes, "Party Politics and the Cultural Revolution," in *Communist China, 1949-69, a Twenty-year Appraisal*, 67.

[9] Shih, 230.

[10] MacFarquhar, 263-264. See also Jean Chesneaux, *China: The People's Republic, 1949-1976*, trans. (New York: Pantheon Books, 1979), 96, 78.

[11] MacFarquhar, 95-96.

[12] Goldman, 19-92, passim.

[13] Robert Scalapino, "The Transition in Chinese Party Leadership," in *Elites in the People's Republic of China*, ed. Robert Scalapino (Seattle: University of Washington Press, 1972), 147.

[14] Goldman, 232.

# Contemporary Chinese Intellectuals, II: Undercurrents Leading to Tiananmen Square, 1980-1988

*Stacey Bieler*

Two events during the Winter of 1979-80 showed the continuing internal tension in the Chinese Communist Party between restricting the intellectuals' freedom of speech and needing their expertise in science and technology in order to strengthen the country. Deng Xiaoping set the limits on discussion with his four cardinal principles in the Spring of 1979: the primacy of Marxism-Leninism and Mao Zedong thought, Party leadership, socialism, and the dictatorship of the proletariat. He also outlined the Four Modernizations — agriculture, industry, science and defense — which required the support and leadership of the intellectuals.

In late 1978 and early 1979 people wrote complaints about the Cultural Revolution on "large character posters" and posted them on the "Democracy Wall," a two hundred-yard stretch of brick at the Xidan intersection in Beijing. But once Deng gained power, he closed down the Wall since the scope of the complaints was broadening from the Cultural Revolution to the Communist Party system. Wei Jingsheng, a former Red Guard and son of a high cadre, put up a large character poster asking that democracy be added as the "Fifth Modernization." He was arrested on March 1979 on "counterrevolutionary" charges and was sentenced to fifteen years in jail. Most older intellectuals did not respond publicly to his arrest. On December 8, 1979 the right to hang posters on the Wall was terminated by the central government.[1]

The following month, an announcement was made that one of Deng's sons, Deng Zhifang, would be sent to study advanced physics at the University of Rochester in the United States. While Deng put restrictions on speech in China, he granted his own son the freedom to study science in the United States.[2]

During the 1980s the Chinese government needed to restore its legitimacy which was in question following the Cultural Revolution. The need for modernization allowed intellectuals to begin acting as a group. Both patron-client relationships as well as new patterns of horizontal connections emerged, which gave intellectuals increased influence. Discussions concerning two ideological issues, Marxism and Westernization, led many to further question the government's legitimacy to rule. The intellectuals, who became more organized in their opposition to Party leadership during the Winter of 1988-1989, and the students' demonstration during the Spring of 1989 caused the government to reset the limits of discussion.

## Intellectual Life During the 1980s

After the crisis of the Cultural Revolution, Deng sought to use economic growth as the way to restore legitimacy and authority of the Communist Party in the eyes of his people and of the world. Most intellectuals did not benefit from the freer economy because they were on fixed salaries during a time of inflation. Their salaries were kept low to remind them that they were not trusted. Newspaper articles described the strain on middle age intellectuals, who had poor health and were dying prematurely from years of mistreatment, yet the government expected them to be the backbone of China's modernization effort. Many began moonlighting. Jokes began circulating about the plight of the intellectuals, such as "It is better to be a barber than a brain surgeon," since a barber was free to set up shop on any street corner. In February 1988 a cartoon portrayed an intellectual daughter as a poor relative in comparison to the daughters who have gone into business.

Intellectuals also lived under another strain, the threat of campaigns. Though Hu Yaobang, Deng's chosen successor, had promised in August 1980 that no more campaigns would be launched, three occurred before June 4, 1989:

1. 1981: The Campaign against Bourgeois Liberalism focused on writers and artists. The primary target was Bai Hua's screenplay, *Bitter Love* or *Unrequited Love*.[3]

2. 1983: The Campaign against Spiritual Pollution focused on famous writers, including Wang Ruoshi for his writings on alienation and humanism.

3. 1987: The Campaign against Bourgeois Liberalism. On December 1986 student demonstrations, which began at the University of Science and Technology (where Fang Lizhi taught in Hefei, Anhui Province), spread to Shanghai and Beijing. The students called for better living conditions, democracy and freedom of the press. Hu Yaobang was blamed for allowing the demonstrations and lost his position as Deng's successor. Three intellectuals, Liu Binyan, Wang Ruowang and Fang Lizhi were blamed for provoking the demonstrations and were expelled from the Party.

The campaigns in the 1980s were different from the Cultural Revolution. Those in the top leadership, some of whom had been victims, did not want to frighten the people again. They also did not want to halt modernization by repeating the ten-year disaster. Thus each campaign was short-lived. Only a small number of intellectuals and specific works were targeted. The masses were not mobilized against the intellectuals. More subtle limitations were imposed, such as closing magazines and banning group meetings. Scientists were allowed to continue working in peace, though the government placed social scientists under tighter scrutiny.

The campaigns continued because different factions within the government disagreed as to how to modernize China. The older "revolutionary generation" leftists still served as patrons to conservative leaders. Moderates pushed for economic, but not political freedom. Radical reformers wanted both economic and political reform. Deng tried to placate the conservatives by setting limits for political or cultural complaints. He skillfully played these factions off one another for his own benefit. He would let one faction win for a while and then rein it in before another faction became too unhappy with him.

## Disunity Among Intellectuals

Chinese intellectuals also broke into factions depending on the different roles they chose to play, their professions, and their age. These three factors generally kept them from making broad alliances.

Intellectuals typically fit into one of three predominant roles. The "Ideological Spokesman" provided authoritative interpretations of the Party's views and policies. However difficulties arose as to whom to support when the leader and the Party began to diverge, as with Mao during the Great Leap Forward in 1960. The "Academic and Professional Elite" wanted to practice their professions without political interference. Though they liked to define "patriotism" as offering their services to the state, tensions increased when it was defined by obedience to the

Party and leader. "Critical Intellectuals" pointed to the shortcomings of the system in order to expose incompetence and corruption, and to convey popular grievances to those in high leadership, in order to help the country function better.

Intellectuals differed on how they viewed their role in society due to the nature of their professions. Since the Party usually felt more threatened by writers than by scientists, the scientists had more support and were allowed more freedom than other professionals. Everyone watched those in literature to feel the temperature of the "winds" coming from the top levels of the Party. One writer said, "When the climate is not good, I translate. When it improves, I write."[4] Film became a weather vane when Bai Hua's *Bitter Love* became the center of controversy in 1981. A quip circulated: An actor said to a writer, "You are fortunate. The people on the Central Committee do not read, but they see films."[5] Studies in fields such as law and social sciences began to recover after years of neglect. Other academic fields, such as political science, public health, economics and education, were encouraged to change their emphasis from being "red" to being "expert" in order to support modernization. An intellectual's profession was often a clear indicator as to the level of controversy he could expect to encounter.

### Generations

The age of an intellectual also affects their view on their role within state and society. A "generation" is defined by "different major historical events, which affected them during their formative years, between seventeen to twenty-five, which still cause them to view life in a certain way."[6] "Generations" is not a precise tool, but it helps us understand what events our Chinese friends in North America are still responding to.

The "Soviet Generation" was studying at universities during the 1950s. [In the 1990s, these are the grandparents who visit North America to care for their grandchildren.] For much of their careers they were in the countryside or jailed in makeshift "cowsheds" in their work units. Having been denied the satisfaction of professional autonomy, they just wanted to be left alone with their work. Most well known intellectuals are from this generation:

1. *Liu Binyin*, (b. 1925) a journalist who wrote about corrupt officials, was kicked out of the Party during the Anti-Rightist Campaign of 1957. After being officially "rehabilitated" in 1979, he gave a talk at a writers convention in November of that year. He said, "Literature is a mirror. When the mirror shows things in life that are not pretty, or that fall short of our ideals, it is wrong to blame the mirror. Smashing a mirror is no way to make an ugly person beautiful, nor is it a way to make social problems evaporate."[7]  In his 1985 essay, "A Second Kind of Loyalty," he argued that a critic could still be loyal. He was expelled from the Party for a second time in 1987.

2. *Bai Hua* (b. 1930), whose story, *Bitter Love*, was about an overseas Chinese patriot who returned to China to help the country after 1949.  After being persecuted for years, his daughter asked him, "You love the country (land), but does the country (government) love you?" The last images of the film show the man wandering through the snow as he was dying. His final steps created a question mark in the snow which raised the question of whether his love for his country was worthwhile.[8] He responded to the 1981 campaign against him by making a self-criticism and retreating to his home.

3. *Fang Lizhi* (b. 1936) was a world-class astrophysicist who spoke to students about democracy. His influence led to elections in the University of Science and Technology in Hefei

which were not prearranged. For years his international reputation protected him from government reprisal. Fang Lizhi was removed from his position at the University and expelled from the Party in 1987.

The "Cultural Revolution Generation" or "Lost Generation" were deprived of their education when the schools were closed during the Cultural Revolution. Many lost their faith in Communism. [In the 1990s these are the older graduate students or graduates now working in the United States.] They feel manipulated and betrayed. Often their "lostness" has made them search for alternative solutions from the West. They are often skeptical of everything. As one friend puts it, "I would like to believe in God, but I once believed in Mao and he failed. It is hard to believe in anything but myself. Please be patient with me."

The "Tiananmen Generation" grew up during the relative economic and political stability of the 1980s. [In the 1990s these are the younger graduate students.] They knew more about the world through television, foreign broadcasts and English teachers than their elders, and they were less connected with their own culture. Before 1989, they were often considered the "Me Generation." One parent said,

> Many young people do not accept [that] there are things in life apart from their own personal interest. They are too selfish and they complain too much about China's backwardness. Instead of comparing China with what it was like before liberation, they contrast it with Japan and the West. They don't appreciate how much better things are now than they were in the old society.[9]

Since much of the intellectuals' power comes from vertical, intergenerational relationships, the process of reforming China was contingent on the healing of divisions between the generations.

## Following Historical Patterns: Vertical Connections

Historically, intellectuals gained power by making vertical linkages with people in high positions of leadership. These patron-client relationships were activated at times of crisis to serve those in power, but they were also career-long collaborations with mutual influence.

During the 1980s, writers found it difficult to have their views known without having a vertical connection to a "backstage" supporting patron who encouraged the writer or groups of writers to say what he would like. The relationship remained ambiguous because the supporter did not want to be too closely accountable for what the writer said and the writer would often use a patron's prestige to press their own views. Intellectuals could make their views known in prestigious publications as long as the patrons were in favor with the government. Although the Propaganda Department controlled all major press and media, a "well connected" journalist or writer could voice an opinion which could influence leadership decisions and public opinion.[10] Liberal-minded editors watched each other, trying to advance or retreat in a well-choreographed dance so no one would be singled out for attack.[11]

All generations felt the "gap." The older generation often did not understand the pain of the "Cultural Revolution Generation" or the selfishness of the "Me Generation," and the younger generations were unimpressed with the sacrifices made by the older generation. One poet, Gu Gong wrote this lament about his "lost generation" son:

> I begin to tremble for my child....Why in the depths of their souls are there such "glacial scars," such "doubt"....I should tell him more about the revolution, the war, and the difficult roads the older generation covered with footprints of blood and tears....I want so

40

much to return him to our generations' way of thinking....In the process of understanding [his] poetry I am understanding my child - the new generation.[12]

In 1986, David Apter, an American professor, visited China in order to study the influence of the early period of Chinese Communist Party (1930 to early 1940s) on youth. After his visit, Apter reflected on the consequence of the "generation gap."

> What was particularly interesting was the almost total divergence in attitude and views between members of the "Yan'an generation" - a remarkable group of idealists, revolutionary puritans, people who considered themselves the founding generation of the Chinese revolution - and younger individuals between the ages of 18 and 26. For some of the latter, Yan'an represented potted [preserved] history, more boring than inspirational. Indeed *it is difficult to avoid speculating on the future political consequences of this divergence.*[13]

While vertical connections were often difficult to make during the 1980s, horizontal connections began to emerge.

## Something New: Horizontal Connections

The goal of modernization forced the Party to exchange its monopoly on decision making for setting policy directions.[14] The intellectuals offered their expertise rather than receiving orders "down from the top." A kind of "consultative authoritarianism" emerged during the 1980s through the growing number of think tanks and Democratic Parties and Groups (DPGs) created by horizontal connections.

Although the DPGs had been disbanded during the Cultural Revolution, they were reinstated around 1980 after the government acknowledged that not all patriots would become socialists.[15] Most DPGs were founded between the late 1920s and early 1940s. After 1949 they were incorporated into the Communist system as bridges to key segments of society, such as scientists and returned overseas Chinese. DPGs had not been permitted to have an impact on the Communist Party, but they were to be impacted by the Party. Several examples of politically-moderate DPGs include: (1) The China Association for Promoting Democracy, mostly school teachers numbering fifteen thousand in 1984; (2) The China Democratic League, with two thousand three hundred chapters (fifty thousand members) in 1984; and (3) The September Third Study Society (*Jiusan*), with twelve thousand higher intellectuals in 1984.

People joined DPGs in order to be with like-minded people, to participate in public affairs outside the Communist Party, to promote China's modernization, or to respond to the Cultural Revolution. By joining these groups they could also help their offspring receive better work assignments and hear inside information before it reached the general public. Though the Chinese Communist Party urged the DPGs to become forums for political advice to the leadership *only* in situations affecting their members or in areas of their expertise, the DPGs gave more than the government hoped for. In 1985, the Democratic League began publishing a monthly magazine with articles about the poor quality of education and they also requested freedom for literary and artistic creativity. Engineers in the Jiusan Society led the opposition to building the Three Gorges Dam after doing a two-year feasibility study. However, the Party still considered the DPGs as beneficial: they could be used as window-dressing so that the Chinese leadership could proclaim that China is a multi-party democracy. Members of DPGs gave their time, money and expertise to help in modernization; and DPGs were used to show a broad base of support for government policies.

Think tanks, which provided support for top-level decisions, were created to ensure that modernization would outlast Deng Xiaoping.[16] They published their ideas in both scholarly journals and newspapers. For example, from 1979 to 1983, a group of high level intellectuals (who had joined the Party before 1949) got together to discuss new economic methods. Task groups studied socialist countries, third-world countries, industrializing Asian countries, and developed countries. They wanted to find out what worked and call it "socialism"![17] "Shadow groups," such as the Beijing Young Economist Society, tried to avoid the limelight. This academic group made radical proposals, such as opening up a stock market, because it was not an organ of the state. After circulating internal documents of the proposals among top Party officials, its official counterpart, the Institute for Economic System Reform published the ideas in its journal, *China Reform*, and in newspapers.[18]

Another shadow group became the most important policy making organ of the entire nation. A small group of younger intellectuals, many of them former Red Guards who spent the early 1970s in the countryside, began experimenting with the responsibility system in a poor county in 1979. The place was so isolated that the changes went unnoticed for a while. As the responsibility system proved to be successful, the group formally gained support from the Secretariat (the most powerful administrative unit of the Central Committee) and was asked to tackle the more difficult task of bringing reform to the cities.[19] Political reform, which was considered much more radical than economic, was also explored. Yan Jiaqi directed the Research Institute of Political Science at the Academy of Social Sciences. He worked in one of Zhao Ziyang's brain trusts, the Research Institute for Reforming the Political System.[20]

The government always feared that intellectuals, when given a chance to act as consultants, would take the opportunity to influence the direction of the country. The leaders felt that they lost legitimacy when they shared control with others. One way the government limited the intellectuals' influence was by forcing them to turn against one another during campaigns in order to save themselves.

## Beginning to Protect Each Other

Historically, intellectuals were called to protect the rights of the people, but they dared not form groups which asserted their own rights of power or freedom. However, in the 1980s intellectuals began to form groups to benefit and protect themselves and to ask for the freedom to hold views which opposed those of the Party.

At the Fourth Congress of the Federation of Literary and Art Circles in 1979, Zhou Yang, an old official in charge of controlling ideological matters in the literary realm, personally apologized to his former victims, writers such as Ding Ling, Wang Meng, and Liu Binyan. Zhou, who had persecuted writers in Yanan (1942) and during the Anti-Rightist Campaign, had himself become one of Mao's wife's victims during the Cultural Revolution. He acknowledged that he had "oversimplified and vulgarized" literature and had "used political authority harshly and rudely."[21]

Professionals began to elect their own officials. On December 1994 at the Fourth Congress of the Chinese Writers Association writers voted by secret ballot for people not on the official slate. Writers who had attacked other writers during the Campaign against Spiritual Pollution in 1983 received fewer votes. In September 1986 the astrophysicist Fang Lizhi argued against the Maoist belief that the workers, not that the intellectuals, were the leading group in society with an essential role in modernization. He called intellectuals to "straighten out their bent backs" and to stop suppressing and attacking one another. Intellectuals followed Fang's admonition during the Campaign Against Bourgeois Liberalization in 1987 and did not speak out against one another.[22]

## Criticizing Marxism

Economic researchers were exploring ways to establish a non-Marxist basis for reform. The campaigns were meant to counteract and contain the debates about Marxism and Westernization that were diffusing from theoretical journals and think tanks to the front pages of the Party's major newspaper and national television.

Intellectuals began reinterpreting Marxism in order to explain why the disastrous Cultural Revolution happened and to seek ways to prevent it from happening again. They also tried to describe why people felt alienated from the Party when it was supposed to represent them. In the early 1980s Wang Ruoshui, a deputy editor of the *People's Daily*, argued that Marxism was a fallible theory rather than absolute truth. He stated that "alienation" grew when "people transfer to the leader powers and dignities which belong to the people." He went beyond blaming the Gang of Four, to blaming *Mao and the whole Party* for the Cultural Revolution. After Deng, in a keynote address on October 1983, warned against the spreading of various forms of "bourgeois decadence" such as humanism, the theory of alienation, "abstract democracy" and modernist literature, Wang Ruoshui was removed from his post. The government's campaigns fizzled by mid-December because it frightened both foreign investors and students studying abroad. Wang returned to the *People's Daily* in late 1984. His popularity with young people was heightened by the way he handled the charges, disdaining to make an about-face or even a self-criticism.[23]

Another aspect of the debate on Marxism was whether or not the conclusions reached by Karl Marx and Friedrich Engels a hundred years before could be applied to China in the 1980s. A "Commentator" article in the *People's Daily* in December 1984 stated, "Many things have happened which Marx, Engels, and Lenin did not experience; we cannot expect people to use what Marx and Engels wrote years ago to solve today's problems." When the article was revised the next day to include "*all* of today's problems," it reflected disagreement within the top leadership.[24]

After being removed from his position at Hefei University in 1987, Fang Lizhi was given a job as a researcher at the Beijing Observatory. His movements were monitored and he was warned to talk only about scientific issues. However he continued to speak about Marxism's failure in China and around the world.

> We are still far behind the rest of the world. And, frankly, I feel we lag behind because the decades of socialist experimentation since Liberation have been a failure.... There is no getting around the fact that no socialist state in the post-Second World War era has been successful, nor has our own 30-odd-year-long socialist experiment.... Clearing our minds of all Marxist dogma is the first step.[25]

In 1988, on the anniversary of the May Fourth Movement (1919), Fang made a surprise appearance at Beijing University, which attracted 500 students. He spoke on freedom and democracy, two ideas which the elderly leaders considered threatening.[26]

## "Culture Fever"

The "open door" policy toward Western influence was the most controversial of all the reforms, especially in light of the loss of faith by many in Marxism. Many within the Chinese government wanted to place a screen across the door. Though they desired Western technology, they feared the ideas, products, and influences that accompanied it. How fine a mesh should and could the screen have? Students and scholars who returned from abroad were directly affected by this controversy because they were seen as carriers of the disease, code-named "Spiritual Pollution" or "Bourgeois Liberalism," which they brought back home along with their degrees and expertise.

The discussion about the nature of Chinese and Western culture was termed "culture fever." Some radical reformers thought that China's history had kept the country from progressing. They felt that Chinese culture should be completely replaced by Western ideas. At the other end of the spectrum were the conservatives who warned against the danger of Western influence and called China to acknowledge its own "spiritual civilization." (Ironically, in all the discussion about the dangers of Western influence, Marxism was rarely acknowledged as also coming from the West!) The moderates wanted to keep what is good from Chinese history as well as embrace certain parts of Western culture. Although all three groups broke into factions because they differed in opinions on the rate and the extent of influence that should be allowed, they all desired to establish a national identity.

Chinese intellectuals compared Chinese and Western culture at conferences and lectures and in journals and magazines. Young scholars associated with the Chinese Association of Social Scientists (CASS) and Beijing University initiated a series of publications under the general title *Culture: China and the World*.[27]

This "culture fever" culminated in the television miniseries, *River Elegy* (*He shang*), screened by Peking Central Television in the spring of 1988. These episodes attempted to establish a historical rationale for the open door strategy and freer coastal economic zones by condemning the traditional land-locked culture of Chinese agriculture. The difference between China's past glories and present problems was highlighted. The Great Wall, the pride of China, was revisioned as a symbol of "confinement, conservatism, impotent defense and timidity in the face of invasion." Initially the series was protected from criticism from those high up in leadership and praised for its voice of "pro-reform." Though Party elders were furious and criticized it for "allegedly vilifying the Chinese people and the symbols of the Yellow River and the Great Wall," Zhao Ziyang was able to block a campaign against the series.[28]

## Organized Opposition

The government's restrained responses to earlier ideological challenges caused intellectuals to become bolder during the Winter of 1988-89. Some complained how academic discussions on humanism and alienation were labeled as political crimes. Others pointed to the need for human rights and democracy as a way to stop the impending social explosion due to public discontent over high-level corruption. Still others called for press laws which would protect the press against lawsuits by corrupt officials. The DPGs began to show more impatience with the government's failure to appoint their members to high-level positions. The Party for the Public Interest, a small party (eight hundred members) made up of returned students, showed its independence by becoming financially independent and deleting from its charter that it was "under the leadership of the Chinese Communist Party."[29]

When those who were advocating democracy began to believe that Zhao Ziyang supported neo-authoritarianism (the belief that an enlightened man could lead China wisely), they became disenchanted with him, and the informal Zhao-reformist intellectuals' alliance fell apart in late 1988. On April 3, 1989 the articles and debates on neo-authoritarianism culminated in a huge forum at People's University. Two thousand students attended the debate where the neo-authoritarians argued that democracy would bring chaos, while those espousing democracy responded that it would ensure stability.

Salons offered another avenue for political discussion and organized political expression. What began as lawn seminars in 1988 at Beijing University (Beida) turned into "democratic salons" which met fifteen times until April 1989. Though Beida's salon is the most famous, independent student organizations at universities throughout the country sponsored informal gatherings. On January 28, 1989 the founders of the *New Enlightenment* opened a salon in Beijing. Publishing only four issues, most of the journal's articles asked why the May Fourth Movement had failed to bring democracy and science to China and exhorted the intellectual community to become an independent force.

Intellectuals also began petitioning the top leaders. On January 6, 1989 Fang Lizhi wrote Deng Xiaoping to request that Wei Jingsheng and other political prisoners be pardoned. Wei's case was particularly sensitive since Deng had personally approved his sentencing. Three petitions followed it:

1. On January 1989, Bei Dao, a poet who had participated in the Democracy Wall movement, organized a group of prominent literary intellectuals to petition for the release of Wei Jingsheng and other political prisoners.

2. Forty-two intellectuals, mostly older scientists, sent a petition on February 26, 1989, proposing political democratization, guarantee of basic rights of citizens, release of political

prisoners and more funding for intellectuals' salaries and for research.

3. Forty-three younger social scientists, humanists, and journalists, including Yuan Zhiming, a writer of *River Elegy*, signed a petition on March 1989.

These challenges to the party's policies by well-known, highly placed intellectuals infuriated both the elders and the reform officials! Zhao Ziyang feared that advocating political reforms would provoke the elders into opposing *all* reforms, including the economic ones established during the 1980s.[30]

## The Aftermath of June 4, 1989

The students mourned the death of Hu Yaobang on April 15, 1989. Though he was a veteran of the "Long March," he was seen as a reformer and protector of intellectuals.[31] The mourning turned into an organized complaint about corruption at high levels and a call for democracy. As the students showed their seriousness through hunger strikes, they gained the support of the townspeople and the unions. The Communist Party leaders felt threatened because *they* had come into power through a combination of students and workers. The leaders lost face when they were unable to properly welcome Mikhail Gorbachev on his first visit to China on May 15 because the students would not leave Tiananmen Square. By May 22, 1989, Zhao Ziyang, Deng's chosen successor and the radical reformers' patron, was stripped of his power. This gave the older "leftists" an opportunity to retaliate against the student upstarts and their political enemies who had been gaining power for ten years. While scores of workers were executed, some intellectuals were jailed. Pictures and descriptions of the "Twenty One Most Wanted" student leaders were televised nationally. Most escaped. Three of the four student leaders were jailed for a year and then allowed to go abroad.[32] Troops were stationed at Beijing's eight major universities. Beijing University's incoming class of Fall 1989 was forced to do one year of military training. Zhang Boli, on the "Most Wanted" list, hid in Northern China as an itinerant farm laborer for two years, became a Christian, and is now receiving seminary training.[33]

Though the older "Soviet Generation" did not march in the streets in 1989, they influenced the younger generations throughout the 1980s by questioning the authority of Marxism. Liu Binyan, who went to Harvard University in 1988 as a scholar for one year, ended up staying in the United States. Fang Lizhi and his wife were allowed to go to the United States after living in the American embassy in Beijing for one year (1989-1990). Seven prominent intellectuals were accused of agitation, including Yan Jiaqi, the political scientist, who was able to escape abroad with his wife. The Writers Association was purged of their top leaders, allowing the old literary officials to retaliate against their enemies once again. The eight Democratic Parties, which had become bolder in their demands during the Spring of 1989, returned to their compliant stance. Works by Fang Lizhi, Liu Binyan, and others were banned. Works about Hu Yaobang and Zhao Ziyang were forbidden. Zhao remained under house arrest.

Some of the "Lost Generation" influenced the students by questioning Chinese culture and promoting Westernization. Members of Zhao Ziyang's think tanks, who pushed for economic reforms, were either arrested or escaped overseas. Chen Yizi, the director of the Institute of Restructuring the Economy, and named as one of the seven intellectuals blamed for agitating students, escaped. Since most researchers in CASS were involved in the demonstration, troops were stationed outside the Academy. One hundred twenty academians at CASS were punished: some were imprisoned while others were dismissed or given warning. Two men, Chen Zhimeng and Wang Juntao, who had established a think-tank called the Social and Economic Research Institute, were arrested in 1989, and in 1991 they were given the longest sentence of thirteen years for sedition.[34] Young professors, who had influenced and defended the students, were removed from their posts. For example, Liu Xiaobo, a lecturer at Beijing Normal University who had written critical articles on Mao and Marxism during the Spring of 1989, was one of three intellectuals who started a hunger strike in order to pressure the government to yield to the students' demands. He was arrested and sentenced.[35] The editors of the major media were purged and replaced with older ideologies. Most of the makers of *River Elegy* escaped to the West. While Yuan Zhiming and Xie Xuanjun have become Christians, others, such as Su Xiaokang have come to appreciate what Christianity has offered to Western society, especially to political culture. Yuan Zhiming is now associated with Overseas Campus, an evangelistic periodical published in California.

## Why Did the Radical Reformers Fail?

Liu Binyan concluded that it was not the students, but the reformers within the Party who lost the opportunity due to disunity. The reformers gave up the initiative (1) for conducting a dialogue between the students and Li Peng's clique; (2) for overcoming their opponents through legal procedures; and (3) of using the modern mass media.[36]

China experts in the West thought that the Chinese leaders had become more democratic because they were allowing some capitalism to jumpstart the flagging economy! Michael Oksenberg, a "chastened China watcher," wrote in *Newsweek* on June 1989: "Four dimensions of the current scene eluded our analytical net: (1) the leadership was even more deeply divided than the outside world understood ...; (2) political reform at the top was superficial ...; (3) an unbridgeable chasm separated the elderly leaders from the youth ...; and (4) the inclusion of China in global telecommunications [meant that] the world watched and through its reaction stimulated both an uprising and its suppression ..."[37]

Some Chinese have found that the basic tenets of Christianity help them make sense of the events at Tiananmen Square. Unlike Confucius who said that men are basically good and became even better if educated, Christians believe that people, who were created good, are fallen. Most leaders continue to hold onto their power no matter the cost. Only by accepting God's love, shown through Jesus' death and resurrection and the indwelling Holy Spirit, can people become unselfish.

Today, most pro-democracy thinkers and activists are quite pessimistic about China's future, despite China's apparent economic success. They perceive that China does not have the social, religious, or political foundation on which to build a democratic society.

## Suggestions for Further Reading
### Introduction to Chinese Politics
Carol Hamrin and Suisheng Zhao, eds., *Decision-Making in Deng's China* (M.E. Sharpe, 1995) especially, chapters 1, 10, 12, 16.

Kenneth Lieberthal, *Governing China: From Revolution to Reform* (Norton, 1995).

### History of China through Intellectuals' Eyes
Lu Shun, *Selected Stories* (Norton, 1960).

Jonathan Spence, *The Gate of Heavenly Peace* (Penguin, 1981).

### Scholars
Liu Binyan, *A Higher Kind of Loyalty* (Pantheon, 1990).

Fang Lizhi, *Bringing Down the Great Wall: Writings on Science, Culture, and Democracy in China* (Norton, 1992).

Orville Schell, *Discos and Democracy* (Anchor Books, 1989) (Part III describes Fang Lizhi, Liu Binyan and Wang Ruowang).

Anne Thurston, *Enemies of the People: The Ordeal of Intellectuals in China's Great Cultural Revolution* (Harvard, 1988).

Yue Daiyun with Carol Wakeman, *To the Storm: The Odyssey of a Revolutionary Chines Woman* (University of California Press, 1986).

## Older Graduate Students, the "Lost Generation"

Tani Barlow and Donald Lowe, *Teaching China's Lost Generation: Foreign Experts in the PRC* (China Books, 1987).

Liang Heng and Judith Shapiro, *Son of the Revolution* (Knopf, 1983).

Jung Chang, *Wild Swans* (Anchor, 1991).

## Younger Graduate Students or "Tiananmen Square Generation"

Andrew Nathan, *China's Crisis* (Columbia, 1990).

New York Times correspondents, *Massacre in Beijing* (Times Books, 1989).

Shen Tong, *Almost a Revolution* (Harper, 1990).

## Chinese Intellectuals in the 1980s and 1990s

Geremie Barme and John Minford, eds. *Seeds of Fire* (Noonday Press, 1989).

Merle Goldman, *Sowing the Seeds of Democracy* (Harvard, 1994).

Perry Link, *Evening Chats in Beijing: Probing China's Predicament* (Norton & Co., 1992).

Su Xiaokang and Wang Luxiang, *Deathsong of the River: A Readers' Guide to the Chinese TV Series Heshang*, trans. Richard W. Bodman and Pin P. Wang (Cornell East Asia Series, 1991).

## Movies on Video

*The Blue Kite* (China in the 1950s/1960s).

*To Live* (China, 1950s to 1970s).

# Notes

[1]Wei was released six months early in 1993, which coincided with Beijing's failed bid to win the 2000 Olympics. After he met with U.S. Assistant Secretary of State John Shattuck in Beijing in early 1994, a court sentenced Wei to another 14 years. He was then released from labor camp and sent to the United States on November 15, 1997. Matt Forney, "Freedom's Price," *Far Eastern Economic Review*, November 27, 1997: 16-17.

[2]Fox Butterfield, *China: Alive in the Bitter Sea* (New York: Times Books, 1982) 415-418. Jonathan Spence, *The Gate of Heavenly Peace* (New York: Penguin Books, 1981) 412.

[3]Merle Goldman, *Sowing the Seeds of Democracy in China* (Cambridge: Harvard University, 1994) 92-93.

[4]Seymour Topping, "Thaw and Freeze and Thaw Again," *The New York Times Book Review*, December 17, 1987: 27.

[5]Ibid., 25.

[6]Michael Yahuda, "Political Generations in China," *The China Quarterly*, 80 (1979) 795.

[7]Liu Binyan, "Listen Carefully to the Voice of the People," in *People or Monsters?* ed. Perry Link (Bloomington, IA: Indiana University Press, 1983) 4.

[8]The cinematic script with related introductory remarks are found in Pai Hua, *Bitter Love*, eds. T.C. Chang, S. Y. Chen, and Y. T. Lin (Taipei, Taiwan: Institute of Current China Studies, 1981).

[9]Beverly Hooper, *Youth in China* (New York: Penguin, 1985) 35.

[10]Carol Hamrin, "Conclusion," in *China's Intellectuals and the State*, eds. Merle Goldman, Timothy Cheek, and Carol Lee Hamrin (Cambridge, MA: Harvard University, 1987) 278-285.

[11]Perry Link, "Intellectuals and Cultural Policy After Mao," in *Modernizing China: Post-Mao Reform and Development*, eds. A. Doak Barnett and Ralph Clough (Boulder, CO: Westview Press, 1986) 90-91.

[12]Gu Gong, "The Two Generations" in *Mao's Harvest: Voices from China's New Generation*, eds. Lelen F. Sui and Zelda Stern (New York: Oxford Press, 1983) 9-16.

[13]David Apter, "China Journey: A Political Scientist's Look at Yan'an," *China Exchange News*, 14.4 (1986): 9, emphasis mine.

[14]Hamrin, "Conclusion," 303.

[15]For this paragraph, I am indebted to James Seymour, *China's Satellite Parties* (Armonk, NY: M.E. Sharpe, 1987).

[16]Mary Lord with Marlowe Hood, "Think Tanks Come of Age," *U.S. News and World Report*, October 12, 1987: 44.

[17]Author's lecture notes from Carol Lee Hamrin's class, Summer 1988.

[18]Andrew Mendelsohn, "Deng's Big Bang: Alvin Toffler in China," *The New Republic*, April 4, 1988: 16.

[19]Harry Harding, *China's Second Revolution: Reform After Mao* (Washington, D.C.: Brookings Institute, 1987) 211. Liang Heng and Judith Shapiro, After the Nightmare (New York: Knopf, 1986) 77-98.

[20]Liu Binyan, *Tell the World* (New York: Pantheon, 1989) 26.

[21]David Kelly, "The Emergence of Humanism," in Goldman, Cheek, and Hamrin, 172.

[22]Li Cheng and Lynn White, "The Thirteenth Central Committee of the Chinese Communist Party: From Mobilizers to Managers," Asian Survey XXVIII, 4 (1988): 395. Orville Schell, "China's Andrei Sakharov, " *The Atlantic*, May 1988: 41. Edward Gargan, "China's Cultural Crackdown, " *The New York Times Magazine*, July 12, 1987: 64.

[23]For this paragraph, I am indebted to David Kelly, "The Emergence of Humanism: Wang Ruoshui and the Critique of Socialist Alienation," in Goldman, Cheek and Hamrin, 166-182.

[24]Goldman, *Sowing*, 136-7.

[25]William Sweet, "Future of Chinese Students in US at Issue," *Physics Today*, June 1988: 70.

[26]David Holley, "Chinese Dissident Surfaces with Plea for Democracy," *Los Angeles Times*, May 5, 1988: Part I, 10.

[27]Zi, 444-448.

[28]Geremie Barme, "TV Requiem for the Myths of the Middle Kingdom," *Far Eastern Economic Review*, September 1, 1988: 40-43. Robert Delfs, "Helmsmen's Lost Bearings," *Far Eastern Economic Review*, October 27, 1988: 37. Goldman, *Sowing*, 259.

[29]*Hong Kong Standard*, December 9, 1988: 6. Foreign Broadcast Information Service (FBIS), December 9, 1988: 23-24 in Goldman, *Sowing*, 274.

[30]For this section, I'm indebted to Goldman's chapter "The Beginning of Organized Opposition," in *Sowing*, 256-295.

[31]Ibid., 301.

[32]Ibid., 332-337.

[33]Kyna Rubin, "Chinese Political Exiles as Christian Soldiers, " *The Asian Wall Street Journal Weekly*, October 10, 1995: 16.

[34]Goldman, Sowing 338-354; For full biographies of the two men, see George Black and Robin Munro, *Black Hands of Beijing* (New York: John Wiley and Sons, 1993).

[35]"Dissident in the Dock?" *Far Eastern Economic Review*, October 26, 1989: 138.

[36]Liu Binyan, *Tell the World*, 104-108.

[37]Michel Oksenberg, "Confession of a China Watcher," *Newsweek*, June 19, 1989: 30.

# From Enlightment to Exile

## Liu Xiaofeng
### Translated by Samuel Ling

*(Editors' Note: This is a transcript of an address given by Dr. Liu Xiaofeng to a meeting of overseas Chinese Christian leaders on April 1990. Liu was asked to survey the various schools of thought among China's elite intellectuals during the decade of reform leading up to spring 1989. While many of the schools and groups became defunct after 1989, it is a significant portrait of the incredibly open atmosphere of exploration under the tutelage of Zhao Ziyang and other leaders in the 1980s. To preserve some of the flavor of the original address, the translator has not tried to reconcile names and references with those which appear in other chapters in this book. This article first appeared in China Horizon, 1:3 (Fall 1990), 7-12.)*

## Schools of Thought Among Chinese Intellectuals

In Beijing, intellectuals gather around six or seven groups. Every one of them has experienced a split of some kind.

### The Culture Academy School (Wen hua shu yuan pai)

Started around 1987, this group is led by a Daoist scholar working with several Beijing University graduate students in traditional Chinese philosophy. They established an independent institute, the Chinese Culture Academy (*Zhong guo wen hua shu yuan*). Their aim is to preserve and promulgate traditional Chinese culture. They do the teaching themselves. Tens of thousands of students, including cadres, enroll in their correspondence courses.

## The "Towards the Future" School (Zou xiang wei lai pai)

Led by a historian, this group's aim is to introduce modern western culture to China, and to advocate the reform of institutions in Chinese society. Their book series, entitled *Zou xiang wei lai zhong shu*, is made up of translations in economics, ethics and other subjects. One hundred volumes have been published. Their magazine, *Zou xiang wei lai*, is the forum where their own views are expressed. Four issues were published before June 4, 1989.

## The Beijing Youth Political Academy School

This group is nicknamed the Youth Party (*Qing nian dang*) among the intellectuals. Their base, the *Beijing Qing Nian Zheng Zhi Xue Yuan*, was formerly the Chinese Communist Youth League Central College (*Zhong gong qing nian tuan zhong yang tuan xiao*). The school changed its name after the Cultural Revolution and was reconstituted after 1985. Their main work is to use the cultural media, such as reporting literature (*bao gao wen xue*) and television, to do concrete reporting of current events. Their target audience is the ordinary masses and those with only an elementary education. Their leaders have produced the famed television series *He Shang* (River Elegy).

## The Beijing Social and Economic Development Research Institute (Beijing she hui jing ji fa shan yan jiu suo)

Established with private funds this group is an independent research institute, with autonomous planned topics and approaches of research. A group of scholars work in this institute, mainly in the fields of political science and sociology. They do pure research and questionnaire surveys are conducted. Concrete abundant data has been gathered in areas such as marriage and family. This is a very talented group and includes members of the think tank surrounding Zhao Ziyang. Early in 1989, a seminar was held in Shenzhen where concrete steps for social reform were proposed.

## The *"Culture: China and the World"* Committee (Wen hua: Zhong guo yu shi jie wei yuan hui)

This group is centered around the Chinese Academy of Social Sciences (*She hui ke xue yuan*) and Beijing University's Philosophy Department. It is a more broadly based organization, and is often regarded as the "intellectual elite" (*zhi shi jing ying*). Their studies include philosophy, religion, literature, history, and law. Their goal is to establish the foundational base for Chinese culture.

Their major effort is to translate the classics of Western scholarship. They also engage in research and attempt exchanges with overseas scholars from Taiwan and Hong Kong, and Europe.

The group is creating a book series called Academica (*Xue shu wen ku chong shu*). Some fifty volumes have been published, mostly translations in five categories:

1. Philosophy (e.g. Martin Heidegger and *Beijing and Time*)

2. Sociology (e.g. Max Weber and Talcott Persons)

3. Theology (especially basic systematic theology texts in modern Western Christianity, including Roman Catholic, Protestant, and Orthodox authors. It does not include biblical theology though)

4. Literature and Aesthetics

5. Anthropology, Psychology, and Ethics

In addition to this serious effort, the group publishes the New Knowledge series (*Xin zhi wen ku*). These are smaller books on sociology, political science, economics, and literature (e.g. Martin Buber's *I and Thou*). One hundred titles have been published so far.

Thirdly, the group publishes a magazine called *Culture: China and the World*. Viewpoints are presented from the writers' own research. Five issues have been published, with the fourth issue dealing with religion such as Christianity and Buddhism.

Lastly, the group publishes the Humanities Research Series (*Ren wen ke xue yen jiu cong shu*). These are works of research done by the scholars themselves, including the intriguing treatment of Christianity, in *Zeng jiu yu xiao yao* by a philosophy professor at Shenzhen University.

## The Transcendentalist Group

This group split from the "Culture: China and the World" School around late 1988. They believe that culture and transcendence (i.e., the spirit, *jing shen*) are two different matters. Their magazine is called *Jing Shen*. Their interests include philosophy, theology, aesthetics, and sociology.

The six schools above have held joint colloquia. There were tendencies toward convergence, but due to leadership and lack of funds, they all have either split or have discontinued some of their projects.

## Chinese Intellectuals and the Christian Religion

The study of religion and China is engaged in several directions:

### The Study of Religion

This approach takes the study of religion as the primary task and usually centers around graduate studies in universities. Their books offer sociological, anthropological, and cultural perspectives on religion. No religious faith on the part of the scholars is implied.

*The Institute for the Study of World Religion* (Zongjiao yan jiu suo) *of the China Academy of Social Sciences* (Zhong guo she hui yan jiu yuan)

This group is closer in scope to Christianity, and has begun a book series on the study of Christian culture (*Ji du jiao wen hua xue*), such as religion and literature, and the works of Paul Tillich. This group includes people who have come to Christian faith.

## Research on Christianity (Ji du jiao yen jiu)

Based in Chengdu, this group's starting point is a firm conviction about Christianity. Their concern is how Christianity can be a concrete social and cultural experience in China. They attempt to firmly root Christianity in Chinese culture in literature, philosophy, and sociology. They have done translations of works by sociological theorists Emil Durkheim, Max Weber, and Peter Berger.

## The Study of Theology

This group's interest is the study of theology (as distinct from the philosophy of religion) and the study of religion. Their focus is the development of Christian theology in the twentieth century, from Karl Barth to Robert Bultmann. They also study Roman Catholic theologians, such as Karl Rahner and Hans Küng, and Eastern European theologies. Their aim is to work with those who are Christians and those who are interested in Christianity.

Two volumes in their book series have been published. Their periodical is called *Ji du jiao wen hua ping lun* (Christian Culture Review). Two issues have been prepared. They are seeking to organize the China Society for the Study of Christianity (*Zhong guo ji du jiao yan jiu hui*), under the auspices of the China Society for the Study of Religion (*Zhong guo zong jiao xue hui*).

Unfortunately, there is no dynamic intellectual force in the church in China, and there is a definite lack of manpower to do scholarly research and writing. The future of theological writing and religious studies requires a lot of concentrated effort.

## Intellectuals In Exile

There are two kinds of Chinese intellectuals-in-exile. First, there are those who are exiles by choice. Many left China before June 4, 1989, and are now in the United States. At some point, if a movement (*feng chao*) occurs in China, they will go back. Secondly, after June 4, 1989, many intellectuals were forced to become exiles.

What kind of culture can these intellectuals create? If we look at the Russian exiles, we see that they created a very rich "exile culture" (*liu wang wen hua*). They were involved in very deep reflective thinking. Some of them have even turned from Marxism to Christianity. They began with culture itself and reached out to a broad societal dimension (e.g. Paul Tillich and the Frankfurt School).

China does not have such a dynamic because the underlying spiritual dimension (*jing shen*) is too weak. Is it too much to ask the Chinese intellectuals to consider a new transcendence after their disillusionment with the transcendence of the socialist utopia? What will be their future development as these "intellectuals in exile" interact with the broader world of Western scholarship, and particularly, Christianity? What will be the role of overseas Chinese Christians in this interaction?

# Starless, Speechless Night

*Translated by Samuel Ling*

*(Editors' Note: These poems were mostly written and published in China and Hong Kong, on or shortly after June 4, 1989.)*

## Reply

### Bei Dao

Despicable - the despicable person's passport,
Noble - the noble person's epitaph.
Just watch, in the gold-plated sky,
Float the bent shadows of the dead.

The ice age is long gone,
Why are there icebergs everywhere?
The Cape of Good Hope has been discovered,
Why are there thousands of sailboats in the Dead Sea?

I came to this world
With only paper, rope and my shadow.
In order that before the verdict,
The voices of the sentenced may be heard:

I tell you, world,
I - won't - be - lieve!
If you have trampled a thousand challenges under your feet,
Count me as Number 1001.

I won't believe that the sky is blue;
I don't believe that thunder is an echo;
I don't believe that dreams are false;
I don't believe there is no retribution at death.

If the ocean was destined to break the dam,
Let all the bitter waters pump into my heart.
If the earth was destined to rise,
Let humankind choose anew the peaks of existence.

New turning points and the twinkling stars
Decorate the coverless sky.
Those are the five thousand year old pictograms,
Those are the staring eyes of a future humanity.

(Written after the Tiananmen Square incident of April 1976.)

*(Editors' Note: Bei Dao, born in 1949, participated in the 1976-1979 Democracy Movement. Students at Tiananmen Square knew his poem by heart. He now lives in exile in the United States.)*

# A Sea of Blood-Red Flowers in May
## Bai Hua

In my eyes, you all grew old long ago,
Your path of youth intercepted at twelve;
Because countless ancestors' corpses
sprang out of the earth,
Leaving pitiful caves for posterity.
Bending over, every step was hard for you to take,
You let sorrow carve its wrinkles
on your infantile foreheads.
Beards, long as the storm,
Backs, fragile as the reed.
At the same time, I thought there will be
no more Mays in China,
There will no longer be enough blood
to stain every young cheek red ...

When you suddenly stepped out so boldly,
I floated along in May -
like a sea of blood red flowers,
You aren't old and senile,
It is I, it is my eyes.

# The Rediscovery of China
## Bai Hua

May, the world in shock turned its eyes to the East.
Innocent, rustic faces of childhood.
Hungry and thirsty, they stood up feebly,
They rolled up and laid on the square their grandfathers ran and
shouted on seventy years ago.
By chance, a flower under the rainstorm struggled to raise its head,
Its bloated mouth said in silence:
Do you know us? We are China.
You are China? The very ancient China?
So young, beautiful, and touching today!
In hunger and weakness, an unshakable strength shows.
Suddenly, all the world's bed became concrete,
All the dining tables of the world became bare and penniless.
Every child in the world learned one sentence of simple Chinese:
Mother, I am hungry.

# Resurrection
### Bai Hua

For God, who emptied his blood on the cross,
Death is the extinction of a prolonged ache,
The embodiment of the experience of human suffering,
The final completion of that great, compassionate will.

For that blade of grass, which fell finally in the snowstorm,
Death is the ultimate insult under torture,
A fierce rage that refuses to close its eyelids,
The accumulated experience of resistance,
ten thousand times over.

But God and grass will yet live again.
When the spring rain floods from the eyes of the people to the
earth,
God steps down from the cross with a smile,
The blade of grass straightens its weak yet resilient back,
Resurrection shall be a solemn holiday;
Songs of celebration, like life, everywhere.

June 6, 1989  Shanghai

*(Editors' Note: Bai Hua was born in 1930. His screenplay,* Bitter Love, *was criticized in 1981 during the Campaign against Bourgeois Liberalism.)*

# The Day There Were No Cigarettes
## Wang Dan

The day there were no cigarettes
I wasn't by your side
But in my heart
You were always my everything
My only one hope
It's dark now, the road cannot stretch to dawn
All my thoughts, one by one, were paved on
The street in that gray, small town
You probably don't like it when no blue doves fly
No cigarettes in hand
So light up a match, smoke your helplessness
Smoke that which will never return
Drizzling ...
When you think of me
There'll be no more days for cigarettes

*(Editors' Note: Wang Dan was one of the "Twenty-one Most Wanted" after Tiananmen Square 1989. He was tried on February 1991, sentenced to jail, but he was released and now lives in exile in the United States.)*

# A Little Poem

Anonymous

Child:       Mother, Mother, why don't these uncles and aunts eat?
Mother:     They want to receive a beautiful gift.
Child:       What gift?
Mother:     Freedom.
Child:       Who will deliver this beautiful gift for them?
Mother:     Themselves.

Child:       Mother, Mother, why are there so many people on the square?
Mother:     This is a festival.
Child:       What festival?
Mother:     A festival to light the fire.
Child:       Where is the fire?
Mother:     In the heart and soul of every person.

Child:       Mother, Mother, who rides in the ambulance?
Mother:     A hero.
Child:       Why is a hero lying down?
Mother:     So the child in the back row can see!
Child:       For me to see?
Mother:     Yes.
Child:       What will I see?
Mother:     A rainbow-colored flower.

*(A conversation between a four year old girl and her mother.)*

## We're All Weeping
### Anonymous

We're all weeping,
Because the sun deserted us,
The earth is full of dry leaves,
The sky suffocates with cloudy rain.

We're all weeping,
Fresh air stained with mud,
A young child is no longer innocent,
The weather-beaten old man shuts his eyes tightly.

We're all weeping,
The white snowflake has lost its truth,
These days the moon is sleepless,
Who will grant us
A song of integrity?

We're all weeping,
The forest doesn't believe the earth,
If sea water irrigates the field,
Our hearts will wither into a saltfield.

We're all weeping,
Weeping cannot change this century,
To seek a diamond-like sunshine,
Courage like the mountain and river we need.

# I Won't Believe

Anonymous

I won't believe
A despicable lie
Repeated a hundred times, a thousand times
Will become the truth
And can cover up
The eyes of the universe

I won't believe
Extra-strength detergent -
A thousand, ten thousand kinds -
Will wash away
That animal look,
Those bloody hands

I won't believe

Justice will be frozen
By white terror
The wheels of history
Will turn backwards to
The palace of feudalism

I won't believe

A fence woven with bayonets
Can be everlasting
A mad beast -
The enemy of one billion people - will triumph

The times have taught me
I
        WON'T
                    BELIEVE

June 4, 1989
*Wen Hui Pao* (Hong Kong), June 11, 1989

71

# Three Poems
### Han Shan

#### I

My younger brother died
My younger sister died
I never kissed them
I never embraced them
They died
My younger brothers and sisters died
Those I've never met
Pierced by bayonets
Struck down by bullets
Flattened by tanks
Their fresh blood
Stained Tiananmen Square red

#### II

Afraid?
Let me hold your hand
It'll be over soon
It won't hurt much
I said weeping

#### III

They fell, bleeding my blood
They fell, shedding my tears
A late-night special report on television
Announces my death a thousand miles away

*Seng Tao Jih Pao* (Hong Kong), June 9, 1989

# When One Person Falls
Wen Xuan

When one person falls
Then a name
Rises
Becoming a tree
Then we will have
Thousands of trees
Maybe even more
Trees
On Tiananmen Square
Along Changan Avenue
Spread out

Giving shade
Children of a later generation
Will no longer fear without reason
Will no longer need to play
Beneath tanks and guns
No more midnight
Rude bangings at the door
They will grow up
With their own
Mouths - Not the party's loudspeaker
These children of a later generation
Left their heads
Thank the trees
Giving shade   Spreading out
Along Changan Avenue
On Tiananmen Square
Thousands of trees
Or maybe even more
Trees
They rise    Every tree
Will have a name
When one person falls

June 12, 1989
*Seng Tao Jih Pao* (Hong Kong), July 1, 1989

73

# The Pounding of My Heart
### Wei Daxin (Ngai Tat-sum)

These are times for deep pain
We shut our windows
Each drifts to his own dream
Yet, this night is not for dreams
The stars and the moon take their course
Along the frontier of darkness
I saw your bitter tears
You saw me weep in the wind

These are times for deep reflection
Our faith, is still laid on the table,
Over and over again, exploring a thousand
  calm and cool reasons
Yet, these are hardly times for solitude,
A thousand letters cannot be posted,
The date lingers at June 4

No rain falls outside the window
No words, either, fall from our lips
So we shut the window
Each keeping watch with a room of flickering
  light, a room of loneliness
Yesterday's emotions, leftover rage
Each stuffs the night of nightmares

We have no words for one another
We can only stare at one another ...
For a moment, we lean back to back
And cry our hearts out
We no longer own our own sky
The sky is red, with flickering yellow stars
On this land that is not ours
Should we regret, mourn, or take pride

These are no longer times for sorrow
These are times for deep reflection
These are times of rumors and lies

These are times of white terror
And now, gunshots are heard outside again
I shut my doors and windows tight, I put out my lamp
In silence, I listen to every pounding of my heart

June 15, 1989
*Breakthrough Magazine* (Hong Kong), August 1989

(Translated by Samuel Ling from *A Starless Night in June: An Anthology of Poems (Sui ran na ye wu xing )*, Hong Kong: Breakthrough Limited, May 1990.)

# China's "Apolloses" and the 1997 Crisis for Hong Kong's Theologians

*Ping Cheung Lo*
*Translated by Samuel Ling*

## Apollos in Acts and in China Today

According to Acts 18:24-28, Apollos was a Jew born and raised in Alexandria, Egypt. Alexandria was the most important center for culture and scholarship in the Mediterranean world in the first century. Apollos was well learned, eloquent, culturally groomed, widely read, and competent in debate. He was well informed about the Bible and had received training in the Way of Jesus. He was enthusiastic about sharing Christ with others, and so traveled to Ephesus in Asia Minor to preach. Though he only knew of the baptism of John the Baptist, Apollos was still able to teach about Jesus fairly accurately. Priscilla and Aquila, upon discovering flaws in Apollos' preaching in the synagogue, took him home and explained to him at length the complete truth of God. Apollos then went on to Achaia and vigorously refuted the Jews in public debate, using Scriptures to prove that Jesus was the Christ.

China's "Apolloses" also came from famous schools. They were trained at or lived near Beijing and other cultural centers in China. Some of them received doctoral degrees from Europe. They are well learned, eloquent, culturally groomed, prolific, competent writers, and are well informed about theology.

However, this knowledge of theology did not come from the church or seminary. For various reasons these Apolloses came to admire Christianity and were committed to raise the level of knowledge in China concerning this faith. Thus they began translating Western theological classics into Chinese on a large scale. They were even writing their own works to introduce Christianity to the Chinese people.

However, the Apolloses have not had a great deal of contact with the church. And though their understanding of Christianity may be correct, it may not be adequate. They bury themselves with theological tomes but seldom read the Bible. They interact with other scholars but do not participate in church life. They talk about Christian theology but are detached from the faith community of Christians. They love theology but may not love God. God is the object of their study and thought but He may not be the object of their prayer and worship.

## Liu Xiaofeng

The most outstanding and best known among China's Apolloses is Liu Xiaofeng. Dr. Liu is a native of Sichuan Province. He majored in foreign languages in college and received a master's degree in philosophy from Beijing University. He served as a professor at Shenzhen University and then studied for his Doctor of Theology at the University of Basel, Switzerland. In 1993 he received his doctorate and moved to Hong Kong. Currently he is a research fellow at the Centre on Contemporary Culture at the Chinese University of Hong Kong, and is associated with the research department of the Christian Study Centre on Tao Fong Shan (now called The Institute for Sino-Christian Studies) in Sha Tin, Hong Kong. Liu has published a number of books. *Zen jiu yu xiao yao* (1989) clearly expresses his admiration of Christianity, while *Zou xiang shi zi jia shang di zhen li* (Walking toward the Truth at the Cross, 1990) is a direct presentation of contemporary Christian theology. These two books will make a tremendous impact on Chinese intellectuals.

## Massive Translation Projects

The greater impact of Liu Xiaofeng may not be through his own writings, but through his participation in large-scale projects, particularly translating Western theological works into Chinese. Because of his study at the Foreign Language Institute in Sichuan, he knows many professional translators fluent in English, French, German, and Russian. He also has many friends in Beijing and Shenzhen who are very enthusiastic about his work. He is currently participating in several translation projects:

1. The "Contemporary European Continental Religious Thought" Series (*Dang dai ou lu zong jiao si xiang xi lie*)

2. Since its inception two years ago, eight volumes have been published by Joint (*San lian*) Publishers, Hong Kong. Recently simplified script editions have been published in the PRC.

3. The "History of Christian Thought and Scholarship Treasury" Series (*Li dai ji du jiao si xiang xue shu wen ku*). Eighty volumes have been designated so far for this series. It includes three series, the Ancient, the Modern, and the Research series. The Institute for Sino-Christian Studies on Tao Fong Shan will first publish the traditional script edition; two publishers in China will subsequently release the simplified script edition. Since 1994, seven volumes have appeared so far in Hong Kong. The series promises to proceed at the pace of ten volumes per year.

4. The "Selected Writings in Twentieth Century Western Philosophy and Religion" Series (1991). This series includes

one hundred twelve significant works by Western theologians, and is to be published in the PRC.

These projects are definitely the largest projects to translate Western theological classics into Chinese since the "Christian Classic Series" (*ji du jiao li dai ming zhu ji cheng*).

## Journals on Christianity

Liu Xiaofeng has edited two journals which promote discussion on Christianity:

### *Christian Culture Review* (ji du jiao wen hua ping lun)

This is the first scholarly journal in China exclusively devoted to discussion on Christianity. The first issue was published in 1990; four other issues have since been published as well. Articles were mainly written by PRC scholars. Unfortunately the journal was discontinued due to lack of funding.

### *Pneuma and Logos* (Dao feng)

This journal is published by the Institute for Sino-Christian Studies on Tao Fong Shan. Launched in the summer of 1994, articles in this journal are likewise written mainly by PRC scholars.

In addition to these projects, Liu Xiaofeng has been involved in several activities. A "Religion and Culture" summer seminar was organized in 1994 and 1995 in China. Participation was enthusiastic and the enthusiasm is growing. The research department of the Christian Study Centre, Tao Fong Shan has recently been "upscaled" to become the Institute for Sino-Christian Studies (*Han yu ji du jiao wen hua yan jiu suo*). Liu is the director of academic research (*xue shu zong jian*) and Yang Xi-nan is the managing director. We expect much more fruit from their labors in the coming years!

## Other Scholars

Other scholars in the "Chinese Apolloses" group merit our attention:

### He Guang-hu

He Guang-hu is on staff with the Institute for the Study of World Religions at the Chinese Academy of Social Sciences (CASS) in Beijing. He is an avid follower of contemporary theologians John Macquarrie and Paul Tillich. He is the editor of the "Religion and the World" series (*zong jiao yu shi jie*). Two titles have been published so far, including first-rate works introducing modern Christian thought into Chinese. Professor He has written *Duo yuan hua di shang di guan — er shi shi ji xi fang zong jiao zhe xue gai lan* (Multiperspective Views on God — An Overview of Twentieth Century Religious Philosophy in the West, 1991). He was on the editorial team of *Christian Culture Review*.

### Zuo Xin-ping

Zuo Xin-ping is assistant director of the Institute for the Study of World Religions, CASS. He received his doctorate from the University of Munich, Germany. He has edited *Ji du jiao wen hua mian mian guan* (Perspectives on Christian Culture, 1991), and wrote *Sheng jing jian shang* (An Appreciation of the Bible, 1992), Niebuhr (1992), and *Ji du jiao wen hua bai wen* (One Hundred Questions About Christian Culture, 1994).

## Tang Yi

Tang Yi is a research fellow at the Institute for the Study of World Religions, CASS. He edited *Ji du jiao shi* (A History of Christianity, 1993), and wrote *Xi fang wen hua yu zhong shi ji shen zhe xue si xiang* (Western Culture and Medieval Theological and Philosophical Thought).

## Zhao Dun-hua

Zhao Dun-hua is vice-chairman of the Department of Philosophy and the Department of Religion at Beijing University. He received his doctorate in philosophy from the University of Louvain, Belgium. He published *Ji du jiao zhe xue, 1-500 nian* (Christianity Philosophy, A.D. 1-500, 1994).

In addition to these four people, many other scholars are engaged in projects to introduce Christianity to China. They write broadly and prolifically.

## Other Works on Christianity

The Commercial Press (in China) has published many translations of Christian works, such as *Ye su zhuan* (A Life of Jesus, 1981, 1993); *Zong jiao gai ge shi* (A History of the Reformation, 1992); *Ying ji li jiao hui shi* (A History of the Church in England, 1991); and, *Lu de zhuan* (A Life of Luther, 1989).

# The "Cultural Christian" Phenomenon
# An Overview and Evaluation

Part I: The Historical and Cultural Background to the Emergence of "Scholars in Mainland China Studying Christianity" (SMSCs)

*Cun-Fu Chen*
*Translated by Samuel Ling*

In most regions of the world the study of the history of Christianity, theology, religious ethics, sociology of religion, psychology of religion, and comparative religion is usually the task of the church, the seminary, and the religion and theology faculties of universities. This is not the case in mainland China.

## Religious Studies After 1949

After 1949, and especially from 1950 to 1951, foreign missionaries and Christian workers were expelled from China by the government. In 1952, universities in China were reorganized. Church-related universities were closed down. Departments of Religion no longer existed. Only one philosophy department was left in China — Beijing University (Beida). Not until 1956 did People's University (*Zhong guo ren min da xue*) start a Department of Philosophy; and in the same year, the Chinese Academy of Social Sciences (CASS) organized their Institute for the Study of

Philosophy (*Zhe xue yan jiu suo*). In 1957, Wuhan University and Fudan University began their Philosophy Departments.

Christian studies within the university and research-institute system in China were removed from the scene. In the 1950s and 1960s, only isolated individuals did research in private. In 1965, CASS organized the Institute for the Study of Religion (*Zong jiao yan jiu suo*). But in reality, it was an institute for the critique of religion. During the Cultural Revolution (1966-1976), radicals dubbed it "The Combat Force for the Elimination of Religion" (*xiao mie zong jiao zhan dou dui*).

If we examine catalogues of books and periodicals published between 1952 to 1978, there was not a single article which treated Christianity seriously and objectively. There were only critiques and confessions.

The situation was worse within churches and theological seminaries. Apart from Nanjing (*Jinling*) Theological Seminary and She Shan Seminary in Shanghai, all other schools were closed down in 1952. From 1952 to 1956, there was a basic protection for religious activities. But this radically changed in 1957. A group of church leaders were designated "Anti-Party and Anti-Socialist Rightists": They were "struggled against" and then assigned to labor reform. The "Great Leap Forward" movement and the People's Communes were then launched in 1958. Religious activities were seen as obstacles to the Great Leap Forward, superstitions which adversely affected productivity. The first campaign to eliminate religion in China was launched. The two showcase areas were Wenzhou in Zhejiang Province and Hongtong in Shansi Province. Clergy and laity alike were organized into political "study classes." Many were forced to announce that they had abandoned their religious belief. The second campaign, much larger and better organized than the first campaign, took place during the Cultural Revolution. By the time the "Gang of

Four" fell in 1976, there was hardly a "team of religion studies scholars" in China. Time did not allow the immediate emergence of a new generation of scholars in religion.

## Resurgence of Religion

However the painful experience of those twenty years, especially the decade of the Cultural Revolution, created conditions for the renewed growth of religion. Previously held ideals, convictions, and criteria for value judgments were smashed. But people still needed spiritual support; they still needed to satisfy their quest for faith (*Xin yang*). So they looked to Christianity, Buddhism, and folk religions for answers. However the existing churches, temples, and monasteries could not meet the need of these intellectuals who had been steeped in atheism and Marxism since childhood. The only way was to search for oneself. A whole cohort of intellectuals (*Wen hua ren*) launched on a journey of exploration. A new team of religion scholars emerged in China's academia: They took over part of the functions of the church, the seminaries, and the religion departments of the universities.

This "team" was largely made up of philosophy graduates who did research in philosophy, especially in Western philosophy and religion. In the early 1980s, the majority were graduates of the Department of Philosophy at Beijing University. In 1952 China's institutions of higher learning followed the Russian model and were totally reorganized. Only Beijing University's philosophy department was retained: The philosophy departments of Tsinghua University and Yanjing University were absorbed into it. Philosophy professors elsewhere in China either changed fields or were transferred into Beida's philosophy department. Therefore the strength of Beida's department became unequaled. Their graduates became key leaders in philosophy departments at the other universities.

By the 1960s, People's, Fudan, Wuhan, Zhongshan (Guangzhou), and Sichuan University began to produce their own graduates. CASS' Institute for the Study of Philosophy and Institute for the Study of Religion had their own graduate students as well. These formed the middle-age generation of religion scholars. Since China's universities did not have a religion or theology department (Beijing University started its own in September 1996), almost all the older, middle, and younger generations of religion scholars were trained in philosophy departments. The main training ground was Beida's philosophy department. A philosophy education not only produced scholars in the theoretical study of religion, and hence the study of Christianity, but also scholars studying Buddhism and Taoism. This is a phenomenon unique to China.

## Why Philosophers Turn to Religious Studies

Why is it that Chinese scholars trained in philosophy would naturally, self-consciously, and willingly turn to the study of religion (either as a new discipline or as an addition to their work in philosophy)? Three reasons come to mind.

1. There has always been commonality between philosophy and religion as to the objective of their study, their function, and their mode of thinking. Greek philosophy evolved out of mythology and animistic religion. Greek philosophy, in turn, created the conditions for the spread of Christianity in the Roman world. Medieval philosophy was subordinate to Christian theology. Modern and contemporary philosophers could oppose or support Christianity, but none could circumvent Christianity to address issues in philosophy.

Therefore in one sense, training in philosophy is good training for the study of religion.

2. China's universities eliminated departments of religion, but religion is indispensable to the humanities. In the humanities, an understanding of society, literature, art and ethics, and of people in every country, is impossible without some knowledge of religion. Therefore, courses in both Chinese and non-Chinese philosophy offered in the universities contained a great deal of Christian and Buddhist content. Even the curricula compiled during the Cultural Revolution had to include a discussion of patristics, scholastic philosophy, and contemporary religious trends. Even when these subjects were condemned or "critiqued," students' interest in further study had been aroused. All philosophy students in China must study Karl Marx, Friedrich Engels, and Vladimir Lenin. But Marx, Engels, and Lenin's works were formed in the linguistic-cultural context of the West. A great deal of this involved creation, Original Sin, the Trinity, and the history of Christianity. Therefore, even the Central Communist Party schools and provincial-level Party schools must study Christianity and its canon, albeit through their "interpretation." Under the right circumstances, the study of philosophy created an interest in the study of religion.

3. Students of philosophy, especially the history of Western philosophy, must read original works in Western philosophy. There is much Christian content in these works. Therefore these students are not only fluent in foreign languages, but they are also experts in their own field. Once given the opportunity they could translate Christian works and theological classics of all periods.

Due primarily to these three factors, scholars in mainland China studying Christianity (SMSCs) are mostly graduates of philosophy departments. Other SMSCs are in the fields of history, foreign (non-Chinese) literature, and art. In order to study the history of the West, the history of Chinese-Western relations, the history of the Ming and Qing Periods, and especially modern Chinese history, one must understand Christianity and the history of Christian missions in China. In order to study Western literature and art, and their influence on China, one must similarly deal with Christian and religious art. Once liberated from the cages of the "extreme left," one could join the ranks of the SMSCs.

## Thought Liberation After 1976

The opportunity for such a movement in "thought liberation" came in 1978, as Hua Guofeng was critiqued and the errors of the late Mao Zedong years were condemned during the "Enlightenment" movement.

Deng Xiaopeng was the symbol among the high-level leaders in China. The April 5, 1976 democracy movement was the symbol for the masses. Twenty years of history became the object of spontaneous reassessment. China was caught up in exploring its future direction. Two covert trends became overt: First, leaders inside the Chinese Communist Party, particularly in its upper echelons, suppressed Hua Guofeng and his faction for their errors and strongly urged Deng Xiaopeng to resume his leadership of the Party. Second, intellectuals, especially "theory" scholars who often reflected the temperament and demands of the masses, began to reassess the thought of Mao from an empirical perspective.

From October 16 to November 2, 1978, an all-China conference on the history of foreign philosophy convened, and over two hundred people attended it. This was the first such conference in

China since 1949. "Leftist" tendencies and dogmatism in the study of philosophy were purged in an effort to recover the true face of the history of philosophy. The first target of criticism was the fossilized framework used in the study of the history of philosophy since the 1950s — that the history of philosophy is the history of the struggle between materialism and idealism, dialectics and metaphysics, progress and reaction, and science and religion. The former is always triumphant; the latter is always defeated. Due to the inner relationship between Western philosophy and Christianity as alluded to above, delegates at the conference naturally discussed how to approach issues such as the assessment of Christianity, science and religion, reason and faith, and the material pursuit of humanity and their intellectual-spiritual needs (*Jing shen ji tuo*). Delegates reflected on the error of a simplistic understanding of Christianity in years past and agreed that Christianity must be studied seriously. Late in November 1978, the first conference on modern Western philosophy was held in Taiyuan, Shansi Province. Over one hundred people attended. This conference purged the erroneous dogmas which regarded modern Western philosophy, including the philosophy of religion, as reactionary. Plans were then laid out to study contemporary philosophy.

## Limiting Factors in Religious Studies

During the second half of 1978, various conferences and seminars were held in Western philosophy, Chinese philosophy, history, literature, and art. There was no conference on religion because the clergy in the church was still in labor reform in factories or in the countryside. As of yet there was not yet protection for normal religious activities. In December 1978, the historic Eleventh Party Congress convened. Deng Xiaopeng began to take charge of the Party as Hua Guofeng's public career came to an end. Hu

Yaobang, who was responsible for practical work for the Party, undertook the task of "rectifying" a series of wrongful cases. Some leaders in the religion sector, who were previously labeled as a "rightist," "undesirable," or "historic counter-revolutionaries," were restored to their original posts. A document concerning religion was drafted in 1979, the first since reforms began. Then the famous Document Number Nineteen was issued in 1982. From this point religious activities in China began to develop along a more normal pattern. Most churches began to rebuild their structures and program of activities. However the church — whether Catholic or Protestant, government-recognized "Three Self" or "Patriotic Association" or "free evangelists" (the underground church) — were not equipped like overseas churches and seminaries to engage in research in the history of Christianity, theology, and all the other fields in religion. There were several reasons for this:

1. There was a severe shortage of clergy. Those who were serving were over sixty years old. They could not meet the ministry demands of rapidly growing churches and chapels. A pastor or priest often had to minister in several areas or in several congregations.

2. The government gradually opened up the doors for foreign exchange. At first, Nanjing Theological Seminary was the only one authorized; later the main church (i.e. the locale of the Three Self offices) in each province could receive foreign visitors, but previous permission must be secured from the provincial/municipal Religious Affairs Bureau. In the Catholic structure permission was first given only to Beijing and Shanghai; later churches with provincial Catholic Patriotic Association offices could receive visitors from abroad. When receiving foreign aid, churches could not do so unilaterally. Protestants could receive aid only through the Amity Foundation in Nanjing while Catholics had to work through

Beijing or Shanghai. Provincial-level Catholic Patriotic Associations could not make decisions on their own; approval must be obtained from their superior units. Because of this, it has been very difficult to change the "closed-door" situation since the 1950s. The world of contemporary theology seems very remote: There is a severe shortage of funds and materials for research, therefore a stagnant situation persists in the church as far as religious studies are concerned.

3. Since the 1980s Protestant and Catholic churches, in addition to Nanjing and Shanghai, were given permission to operate their own seminaries (or branch campuses) in each province. At present, their task is to train up a generation of clergy to fill the gap. Theoretical studies in theology and the relationship between Christianity and China cannot yet be on their agenda.

4. Ministers and workers in the church are more conservative than their counterparts overseas. They seldom come into contact with trends in twentieth century theological thought; their mindset makes it hard for them to accept novel ideas. Some younger and more open-minded clergy are dissatisfied with the older leaders, but they have yet to become an influential force.

There are all kinds of factors which make the church and the seminaries in China incapable of taking up the task of Chinese theology (*Han yu shen xue*).

## Religious Publications in the 1980s

The following are some articles on religion published in the newspapers and periodicals in mainland China from 1980 to 1990.

1. The church publishes *Zongjiao* (Religion), jointly edited by Nanjing University and Nanjing (*Jinling*) Theological

Seminary. The Three-Self Movement in Shanghai publishes *Tian Feng* (Heavenly Wind), which has an emphasis on biblical studies.

2. The primary manpower for theoretical studies in religion, criticism of "leftist" tendencies, and oversimplification of religion, comes from the Institute for the Study of World Religions (China Academy of Social Sciences), as well as CASS and university scholars studying Western philosophy and philosophical theory.

3. The two most influential periodicals, both from CASS, are the *Shi jie zong jiao yan jiu* (Studies in World Religions) and the *Shi jie zong jiao zhi liao* (Sources in World Religions). There are also university and local-level CASS journals, *Zhe xue yan jiao* (Philosophical Studies), *Du shu* (Reading), and other national-level periodicals.

4. There are also journals which offer translations of and introductions to overseas trends in religious studies and contemporary theology. In addition to the *Sources in World Religions*, there are the *Zhe xue yi chong* (Philosophy Translation Collection, by the CASS Institute for the Study of Philosophy); *Guo wai she hui ke xue dong tai* (Overseas Trends in the Social Sciences); *Xian dai wai guo zhe xue she hui ke xue wen ze* (Digest of Modern Foreign Philosophy and Social Sciences); *Li lun xin xi bao* (Theory News); *Shang hai she hui ke xue yuan xue shu ji kan* (Quarterly Journal of the Shanghai Academy of Social Sciences), etc.

This list does not include original writings, anthologies, and translations. These three kinds of works have been exclusively produced by scholars outside the church. One cannot blame the church or the seminaries for this phenomenon. The church needs to quickly catch up in the present context.

## The Composition of SMSCs and Their Distinctives

To better consider the historical significance of SMSCs and their relationship with CCs (Cultural Christians), we need to analyze their composition and distinctives. One can analyze the composition of SMSCs from different angles, with different sectors within SMSCs having different distinctives.

### *Background*

SMSCs come from different institutions:

1. Pre-1949 Christian universities in China. There is an extremely small number of SMSCs in this group, and they are very elderly (for example Fu Le-an and Zeng Ju-sheng).

2. University Philosophy Departments before the Cultural Revolution (mainly Beijing University).

3. University History Departments before the Cultural Revolution (for example, Hu Yu-tang and Xu Ming-de).

4. Younger Scholars who graduated after the Cultural Revolution. The caliber of students who entered universities from 1977 to 1979 were particularly high. A new force emerged, mainly in philosophy and history. After 1986 some who majored in religion did research on the theory of religion, Buddhism, Daoism, Christianity, and animism, but there are very few of them, and the fruit of their research is not yet significant. These younger scholars are attracting much attention. Since the late 1980s they have become the new mainstream of SMSCs.

5. Scholars Who Studied Abroad. After 1977 many young graduates went abroad for further study. They enrolled in degree programs in seminaries, religion, and philosophy.

They received formal training in Christian doctrine, contemporary theology, and contemporary religious philosophy; some even had spiritual experiences. They are fluent in foreign languages and understand trends abroad. They returned to China as a new dynamic force. Examples are Liu Xiaofeng and Zhao Dunhua. This fifth group within SMSCs is by nature an extension of the fourth group. Among the fourth group are a good number who have returned from study abroad. This elite corps grew up in the late 1980s and will be a link to the future.

## Age

We can divide SMSCs this way by their age:

1. Those who passed on in the 1980s (e.g. Xu Huai-qi and Hu Yu-tang).

2. The older generation of SMSCs. They graduated between the victory after the Sino-Japanese War (1945) and the Cultural Revolution. They are all over fifty years old. They experienced pre-1949 and post-1949 China, and after 1949, they witnessed or personally experienced all kinds of political, intellectual, or social campaigns, culminating in the Cultural Revolution. In addition, they experienced hunger from 1960-1962 when the Great Leap Forward had failed. Within their own professional fields (e.g. philosophy, history, and literature) they went through a whole series of "criticism campaigns." Great injury had been inflicted upon their souls. Their experiences were deep and painful. They were a generation of eyewitnesses to history. A great number from their ranks would have explored Buddhism or Christianity. Their understanding is penetrating and they are motivated to become involved. Their background is deeply embedded in the contemporary Chinese experience. However, with the small

exception of those who graduated from Christian universities (in pre-1952 China), most of them did not have any background in religion. They studied religion on their own. Therefore they have certain characteristics: they can absorb a great deal of knowledge, their activities are scattered, no one controls anyone else, and, depending on the political climate, they can move about between two or more academic disciplines, or in some cross-disciplinary space. Since they did not originally receive formal training in religion their level of understanding still needs to be raised (with individual exceptions).

3. Middle age SMSCs. This generation has been growing in prominence since the late 1980s. They are the strongest group within the SMSCs. They are around forty years old and went to college during the 1977-1979 period. Yet this group experienced much misfortune. During their high school years, or immediately after high school, the Cultural Revolution broke out. For six years China's universities did not admit any students. According to the policy at that time, all members of urban households were assigned to the countryside (*Shang shan xia xiang*), either in the remote Northeast or Northwest China, or among the rural poor in one's province. Later a regulation allowed parents to keep only one child at home. When these middle age SMSCs entered college and graduate school Chinese society was most open to Western thought. New trends in philosophy, religion, art and literature were introduced from abroad. Given their unique experience, they have a deep sense of agony and hatred toward China's social ills; they work hard to forge a future for themselves, their nation, and their race. Some of them converted to religious faith. The list of articles about religion and Christianity, gleaned from China's periodicals from the 1980s to the 1990s, reveals that they reached a peak around 1977 and 1978, which was called

"Religion Fever." After 1992 a second peak was reached. The younger SMSCs began playing a significant role during these two peak periods. They are strong in sharp thinking skills, youthfulness, high energy level, and a pioneering spirit. Their weaknesses include the lack of experience in society and inadequate understanding of China's complex situation. In China, research into Christianity is a sensitive matter because it touches on modern Chinese history. There are many policies and concrete regulations and even "implementation procedures" and "memoranda" in a particular province or region. A few statements made by a certain leader become the framework to direct a particular geographical area for a particular time. It is easy for these younger scholars, through negligence, to court trouble for themselves.

In addition to the three generations of SMSCs outlined above, there is at present a generation of master's and doctoral students, and college graduates. These young people have an interest to study religion but they are not yet SMSCs. Yet they are the reinforcements for SMSCs; some will become SMSCs, then Cultural Christians. They merit our attention.

## Specialties and Geographical Distinctives

Of all distinctions which can be made about SMSCs, the two above (background and age) are the most significant. We can also analyze them from other perspectives; for example, in terms of their specialties.

1. Those studying contemporary theological theory, and contemporary intellectual trends in religion.
2. Those studying the history of Christianity.
3. Those studying the history of Christianity in China.

4. Those studying contemporary Chinese Christianity and exploring ways in which Christianity can be integrated with Chinese culture.

In terms of regions, we can speak of the Northern and the Southern "Parties" in China. The "South" refers to Shanghai, Hangzhou, and Nanjing. The "North" refers to Beijing, where the graduates of CASS' Institute for the Study of World Religions, Beijing University, and People's University often rely on their relationships with their alma mater or with their schoolmates who stay on in the alma mater to teach, for joint projects in translation, and research. We are not speaking of real "factions" here; we are only making a geographical distinction. However, there are real differences between the two. In general, scholars in Beijing have better access to source materials and more opportunity for exchange with overseas research. They tend to do translations and research into contemporary religious and theological theory. Those in the South, or "out-of-town scholars" (*Wai di xue zhe*, i.e. outside Beijing), focus on practical matters by taking advantage of their regional strengths. They tend to study the history of Christianity in their region and present issues.

## General Characteristics of SMSCs: A Summary

Now let us summarize the overall characteristics of SMSCs. In the context of global realities today and in comparison with church-related seminaries in mainland China, we find the following characteristics among SMSCs:

### Dispersion and Individuality

Compared with scholars in philosophy, history, literature, science, and technology, scholars in China studying Christianity

97

are far more dispersed and isolated. To this date, there has been no conference on Christianity. No mass organization, symposium, or seminar has ever convened. These scholars made a conscious choice, according to their interest, to depart from their field of specialization to study religion. There has only been cooperation in terms of specific projects or activities. In terms of distribution over China, this has been spontaneous since the scholars are all scattered. One knows who exists in such and such a school only from the published results of their work.

There is another external reason for this phenomenon. In order to establish an academic association in China, one must go through a complicated adjudication process. No one has tried to ascertain whether a Society for Christian Studies would be approved. But one can surmise that it will be quite difficult, judging from participation in international academic conferences and conducting activities inside China. People began to hold an inexplicable opinion: Studying the Buddhist scriptures is not dangerous, but studying the Bible and Christianity is because it is associated with Westernization and liberalization.

Even church leaders don't show a positive attitude; in their hearts they don't welcome scholars who study their faith. Therefore, there is only a small number of people who study Christianity. They try not to draw attention to themselves and are even less willing to participate in any corporate activities in order to stay out of trouble. Under such circumstances, Cultural Christians (CCs) who are a product of SMSCs, are not willing to join any church. One could say though there has been some improvement since 1992. For example, Hangzhou University supported the formation of the Hangzhou University Institute of Research on Christianity (March 1991). Activities are conducted as an organization, while non-formal groups meet in other cities.

## Broad Perspectives

Most SMSCs are also scholars in philosophy, history, art and literature. Most of them are adept at foreign languages and can read foreign language books sold in China. They have a high capacity for personal in-depth study, and have engaged in wide contacts and exchange with overseas scholars since the 1990s. They are far more informed than church and seminary leaders on research-related information and worldwide trends. Their uniqueness lies in their broad perspective and quick minds. Their writings are original and thought provoking; their viewpoints on various issues are often new. They are not bound by any denominational framework; they do not repeat outdated slogans.

Yet when in conversation with overseas scholars, they seem short on expertise. Related to this is the fact that their opinions may not be stable; they are easily influenced by new theories in theology or by Buddhism and Hinduism. Therefore in this cultural-linguistic context and intellectual environment, they may emerge as "Cultural Christians," or they may come up with pan-religious viewpoints, mixing Christianity with Buddhism, Daoism, Confucianism, etc. Even if they are "Cultural Christians," it is in more an academic than a religious sense.

## First-Hand Experience in Chinese Culture

By living in mainland China, SMSCs have first-hand experience in Chinese culture, the background of Chinese society, and the Chinese linguistic-cultural context. They maintain good relationships with government agencies which regulate religion, and with churches and Christians on the local level. They have more or less gotten involved in observation and surveying on the local scene. They are equipped to discuss issues related to the in-depth integration of Christianity with the Chinese context and issues related to establishing a theological theory for the Chinese-language world (*Han yu shi jie*). In this, they are in a far better position than overseas scholars, including those in Taiwan and Hong Kong. Since the Chinese government limits local surveying of religion by overseas scholars, this puts tremendous restraints on their research. Since SMSCs do not do their research from the standpoint of Catholicism or Protestantism, they can see things which church members cannot. SMSCs' viewpoints are also different from those of the government. As Chinese citizens and scholars, they strictly adhere to the constitution, the laws, and related regulations. The fruits of their research are also quite valuable to the government.

The composition and characteristics of SMSCs are determinants for the emergence and characteristics of "Cultural Christians." They form a foundation for understanding "Cultural Christians."

## The Historical Place and Role of SMSCs

SMSCs have unfolded a new chapter in exercising these functions, which are beyond the ability of the churches and seminaries in China.

They were able to point out errors and restore the truth. They corrected the "leftist" theoretical errors concerning religion in a way acceptable to the churches and to the government. They have laid a theoretical foundation for the concrete implementation of religious policy.

"Religion is the opium of the people." This was the theoretical foundation for the erroneous "leftists" in matters pertaining to religion in the 1950s and 1960s. For so many years, people took this to be a cardinal truth handed down from Marx. Beginning with Lenin, people held to their conclusions about the nature of religion. In his book *Nation and Revolution*, Lenin said, "There are two tasks for the nations in the ruling class (i.e., the oppressive nations). First, they were executioners (i.e., they suppressed the people). Second, they were pastors (i.e., they numbed the people's consciousness)." From this they deduced another conclusion: "religion is the tool for the ruling class to anesthetize the people." As this viewpoint is put into the Chinese context and linked with the history of China, we see a further development: Christianity is the tool for the Western powers' aggression against China. In 1958, China entered the climax of the Great Leap Forward and the People's Communes movement. The slogan at that time was, "Militarize organization, combatize action, collectivize life, revolutionize thought." Production in the countryside was organized like military units. There was often overtime and night work. Common dining halls were built and everyone ate and lived together. In this context, the cadres in the village and at the *xian* (township) level felt that the Christian worship services and the religious life of ordinary Christians were obstacles to production. A jingle at that time said:

> The Jesus religion hinders collective production; let's add it up, every month you've got to go four times; each day seven points, that's three hundred and three a year; income is slashed, how can we improve our lives? If you want a Great Leap Forward, Jesus, don't ruin our plan.

While in 1958 religion was considered harmful to productivity. During the Cultural Revolution, religion was a detriment to China's politics. Religion was considered as one of the "Four Olds" in that it was a reactionary force. There was "iron-clad evidence" that religion was the opium of the people, so much so that people in the church must willingly or unwillingly accept them. And ever since the movement for thought liberation in 1978, theoreticians began raising questions about the nature of religion. Translators began to investigate into copies of Karl Marx's manuscripts and discovered that these were not the word of Marx, but those of a young Hegelian scholar, David Friedrich Strauss. Judging from its linguistic-cultural context, Marx did not say that this was the nature of religion (i.e., opium of the people). Document Number Nineteen realized the change in theory concerning religion. This basic change is the foundation for other changes in theory and policy. In subsequent developments, SMSCs were often the pioneers in the exposition of theoretical issues. This is the first important function of the SMSCs.

SMSCs translated and introduced major Christian works throughout the centuries, including twentieth century theological theory. They provided information concerning the development of religious studies around the world. SMSCs have taken advantage of the resources available to them at their work units and have engaged in translation or research, openly or otherwise.

In the late 1980s a series of books and translations of Western theological religious works have appeared in China. The translation teams tended to be made up of younger scholars. Some of the works include:

1. *Christian Culture Review* (a journal). Editor: Lin Xiaofeng. Assistant editors: He Guang-hu, Wang Wei-fan, and Zhang Xian-yong.

2. *Selections from Twentieth Century Western Religious Philosophy* (a three volume anthology). Editor: Liu Xiaofeng. Translators: Yang De-you, Dong Yong, et al.

3. *Selections from Twentieth Century Western Religious Anthropology* (a two volume anthology). Editor: Shi Zong. Translators: Jin Ze, Song Li-dao, Xu Da-jian, Chen Zhiping, Chen Guan-sheng, et al.

4. *Religion and the World (Zong jiao yu shuie)* Series General Editor: He Guang-hu.

5. Western Scholarly Series. Published: *History of Comparative Religion*, translated byLu Da-ji, He Guang-hu, and Xu Da-yun.

6. Humanities Series; *Culture: China and the World*. General Editor: Gan Yang. Included in this series is Liu Xiaofeng's book *Zen jiu yu xiao yao*, divergent attitudes toward the world by Chinese and Western poets.

7. Chinese Studies (Overseas). Series General Editor: Wang Yuan-hua. Published: *China and Christianity* (Paul A. Cohen), translated by Di Sheng.

8. *The History of Christian Thought Academic Treasury*. Published by Tao Fong Shan Christian Study Centre (re-named: Institute for Research on Chinese Christian Culture - *Han yu ji du liao wen hua yan jiu suo*). Three series within this series: Ancient, Modern, and Scholarly research series. General editor: Liu Xiaofeng. Translators are all from mainland China.

In addition, journals such as the *Shijie zongjiao zhiliao* (World Religion Resources) began to publish new achievements in overseas religious studies and theology. *Ershi shiji wenku* (Twentieth Century Treasury), published by Joint (*San lian*) Publishing Company of Shanghai, has likewise included translated works in religion and philosophy. These proved extremely valuable for churches, Christians, and non-Christians in terms of understanding historical Christian documents, the fruits of recent scholarly work, and the establishment of religion and theology in the Chinese linguistic context. Many young people developed an interest in studying Christianity as a result of reading these works.

SMSCs have collected, processed, and compiled materials on the history of Christianity in China. They are studying the history and future prospects for the propagation of Christianity in China, the possible ways in which Christianity and Chinese culture may be integrated, and the theoretical basis for Christian theology in the Chinese linguistic-cultural context (*Hanyu wenhua quan*).

Many churches and seminaries inside and outside China are engaged in this work. Concretely, there are several types of work:

1. Gazettes (*Fang zhi*). Since the 1980s, with the support and organizing efforts of the Chinese government, various provincial, municipal, and township (*Xian*) governments have established "*fang zhi* compilation and editorial committees" in order to publish *fang zhi* for the township, city, or province. At present, over half of the townships (*Xian*) in the provinces of Zhejiang and Fujian have published their own *Xian zhi*, which included an introduction to religion. People from all sectors of society participated in these projects, including many SMSCs. It varies with each location.

2. Religion departments in the government have organized church leaders to write local gazettes on religion (*Zongjiao zhi*). Two parts of the *Zhejiang Zongjiao Zhi* have been published, providing an overview of Catholicism in Zhejiang and a survey of Buddhism, Daoism, Catholicism, Protestantism, and folk religion in the city of Wenzhou. This project was undertaken mostly by members of the church.

3. The collection, processing, compiling, and research of specialized materials on the history of Christian missions in the Ming and Qing Periods. This project is undertaken mainly by SMSCs (e.g. Xu Ming-de, Lin Jin-shui, and Tao Fei-ya). Such efforts will make a long-term contribution to both the government and the church.

4. Study on the history of Christian missions in China, especially on the integration and conflict between the two different cultures as Christian missions encounter Chinese culture. For example, Yang Shi-zheng and myself are in the middle of such a project.

5. Study on the traditional Chinese view of God and exploration into the establishment of Christian theology in the Chinese linguistic-cultural context (*Han yu wen hua quan*). This is the focus of attention of scholars both in and outside the church. Liu Xiaofeng has made a tremendous contribution in this area.

6. Study on the current development of Christianity on mainland China and exploration into development trends in Buddhism, Daoism, Christianity, and folk religion in China's modernization process. The study of various theoretical questions which have emerged in the present spread of Christianity in China from the perspectives of theology, religious ethics, and the sociology of religion. This is a main topic of research on the part of the Hangzhou University Christian Study Centre.

7. The six types of projects listed above are not all of the accomplishments of SMSCs. There is no doubt that SMSCs have made great contributions in the area of religion in China, particularly the inroads made by Christianity in the country.

Beyond these three types of activities, SMSCs have also sought to be communication channels between government agencies which regulate religion and the church. They have helped the government and the church in the preservation of documents and artifacts related to the history of missions, the repossession of church property, the search of materials lost during the Cultural Revolution, and offered positive help to the churches.

## The Relationship Between the SMSC Phenomenon and the "Cultural Christian" Phenomenon

The study of the SMSC phenomenon is the foundation for the study of the "Cultural Christian" (CC) phenomenon. This is true especially during the present stage, as the CC phenomenon is not yet fully developed while the SMSC phenomenon is. From the viewpoint of research methodology, the emphasis obviously should be placed on the SMSC phenomenon and this is the approach we are taking. Through the four kinds of analyses above, we can make the following conclusions concerning the relationships between the SMSC phenomenon and the CC phenomenon.

CCs form the nucleus of SMSCS, or at least are the most important part of SMSCs. SMSCs and CCs sustain an extensive and mutually inclusive relationship, and not a cross-relationship. That is to say, CCs are first and foremost scholars in mainland China during the 1980s and 1990s who studied Christianity. They are not from some social stratum outside this circle of SMSCs. Therefore, they share the same historical and cultural background with SMSCs.

The question which remains is: Why did the CC phenomenon emerge from the SMSCs? Against what kind of historical and cultural background would a portion of Chinese scholars, poets, or artists who study Christian culture move on to identify with and trust in Jesus Christ? This is a more complicated question. External factors contribute to it. For example, social change, the spread of Christian documents and theological works, and the development of the Christian church in China, have explained this trend. There are also internal factors, such as an individual's circumstances and experiences, and the inner responses of the soul. It is still difficult at present to do an in-depth study, because the CC is such a new phenomenon and there are still very few of them. And among this small number, very few are willing to identify themselves publicly.

SMSC is the soil which produced CCs. The unique historical conditions in mainland China will inevitably produce a cohort of scholars who would study Christianity and at the same time love Christian culture. Even in the absence of seminaries and academic departments of religion, there will be a group of people studying Christianity through other humanistic disciplines. The most important insights to be gained through this phenomenon at present are:

First, the CC phenomenon has deep historical roots. It is understandable why some people, whether in China or overseas, would deny that CCs are in fact Christians. However it is contrary to the fact to deny their existence.

Second, the SMSC is the foundation for the existence and development of CCs. The broad-based scope of SMSCs activities made it possible for CCs to move about and engage their talents.

Third, SMSCs can no longer be rooted out. This means that CCs will not disappear either. On the contrary, as SMSCs continue to expand, CCs will also continue to develop.

The composition and characteristics of SMSCs include some of the composition and characteristics of CCs. The place and roles of SMSCs also reveal the fundamental place and roles for CCs. In other words, even though people deny the existence of CCs, especially the place and role in Chinese society, they cannot deny the place of CCs as the very backbone of SMSCs, and the roles played by CCs. Of course, as Cultural Christians, they have unique characteristics and status which are different from those of SMSCs. But such unique characteristics can be identified and studied only after the ranks of CCs have been expanded further and have displayed their value. It is difficult to draw conclusions at the present time.

Because CCs and SMSCs sustain the above threefold relationship, and because CCs are often core members of SMSCs, CCs are often the core strength, organizers, and leaders within

SMSCs. As stated above, SMSCs are individualistic and dispersed. They are short on materials and funds for research. They need someone to organize research projects or academic activities. There are some who are playing this role in China today. One cannot say that those who play this role are the CCs. However, one can say that some of these leaders are CCs or potential CCs.

This is a preliminary report regarding the historical and cultural background of SMSCs and CCs. There are bound to be deficiencies. But we believe that this is a very good beginning because SMSCs and CCs are both very important groups in China today. They have a bright future for development and growth. Therefore any study to understand them will have great potential in the coming days.

## Part II: The "Cultural Christian" Phenomenon in Immediate Context, With Theological Reflections

### Edwin Hui
### Translated by Samuel Ling

The concept of the "Cultural Christian" (CC) is an old concept, though usage and definitions vary. In the late 1980s, the term referred to scholars in mainland China studying Christianity (SMSCs) as defined in the first half of this chapter. Dr. Liu Xiaofeng of the Institute for Sino-Christian Studies has given the concept a new interpretation. Between 1988 and 1989, Liu published ten articles under the theme, "Glimpses at Twentieth Century Western Theology" in *Du shu* (Reading) Magazine. Through these articles the concept of "Cultural Christians" began to take shape.

For years *Du shu* had enjoyed a solid reputation and exerted a considerable influence in China, enjoying a large circulation, taking an open intellectual stance, and practicing freedom of opinion. Authors in this magazine usually expressed their personal insights or analyses, exposed or critiqued contemporary phenomena, and raised issues in need of deep reflection, through introducing, evaluating, or translating some work by a well-known author. Although Liu did not formally mention the concept of "Cultural Christians" he clearly commented on the meaning of the phenomenon which was to unfold shortly thereafter. For example, when introducing the "ecumenical theology" of Hans Küng, Liu supported the transcendence of Roman Catholic — Protestant differences or those between Protestant denominations. He favored an end to confrontation and a renewed practice of unity, supporting those who refrained from joining a church or a denomination.[1] In an article commemorating Dietrich Bonhoeffer, Liu wrote regarding our participation in the suffering of God by saying: "It is most enlightening that Karl Barth distinguished between God and religion-or between God and Christianity itself. Barth made it clear that, as a religion, Christianity may become extinct at some point in time; but God exists eternally." While commenting on the concept of "religiosity" in Bonhoeffer, Liu made some very significant remarks: "A Christian does not need to religionize (*Zong jiao hua*) himself; he does not need to put on the cloak of religion. Faith is the action of life in its entirety. Therefore, becoming a Christian does not consist of holding to religious formalities, but in living concretely and positively participating in the suffering of God in this life, in this world."[2]

In 1995, as we will see later in this article, Liu developed this concept further. He defined "Cultural Christians" as those with faith in Jesus Christ and active participation as Christians, yet without being baptized or joining a particular church or denomination. They are above churches and denominations.

Liu, in appreciation of Leo Tolstoy's works, wrote an article called "Hearkening and Mystery." In it Liu wrote: "In our hearts, there is an inner, deep faith in the basic doctrines of Christianity,"[3] and the Chinese people are no exception.[4] Liu affirmed that "in [Karl] Rahner's transcendental-existential theology and anthropology, when man, at a concrete point in history, realizes the essence of humanity, or the true essence of man reaches perfect humanity, that is, being a Christian, it is not important whether he himself knows this." According to Rahner, the common demand of Christianity is: "to be a Christian is to be human in concrete reality; to be truly human is to be a Christian anonymously.... In light of this, the transcendence and the Christian-ness of man can be expressed in different ways, under different names."[5]

In 1990 Liu revised and expanded these ten articles and added three more to publish *Zou xiang shi zi jia shang di zhen li* (The Truth which Walks toward the Cross). The volume was released by Joint (*San lian*) Publishers in Hong Kong. The purpose of this work was to digest the rich history of twentieth century Western theology and to build a Christian theology in the contemporary Chinese linguistic-cultural context (*Han yu ji du shen xue*). He believed that this task could not be achieved by a single religion or denomination; rather, it would require participation by all theologians and scholars sharing a common purpose. In this participation, scholars who can transcend churches and denominations, while maintaining a firm faith in Jesus Christ, can exert a special influence. This type of scholars has a special meaning in the twentieth century, a century in search of "uniformity" (*I ti hua*), especially in China which has gone through tumultuous institutional changes in recent decades. Thus Liu's book sought to introduce to the Chinese people this type of theologian and theological ideas.

For Liu Xiaofeng, "Simone Weil is a Christian; furthermore, she was a great Christian. Yet, because Weil had consistently refused baptism and refused to receive the Sacraments, she placed herself outside the church and outside Christian institutions. This makes her identity as a Christian, at least in its formal meaning, problematic."[6] Liu further wrote: "She is a truly qualified Christian, or she is more of a Christian than some Christians who bear the name formally."[7] As these thinkers are introduced, the concept of "Cultural Christians" takes shape more clearly. Liu took the further step of identifying CCs by name: "There is the

Christian theology which does not belong to any order or denomination, for example the theology of Cultural Christians (e.g. the theology of Solovyev, Weil, and Kierkegaard)."[8]

There were no responses from mainland China to the "Cultural Christian" concept. However, the response from outside China was considerable.[9] The term "Cultural Christian" met great resistance from members of the Christian church in Taiwan and Hong Kong. Some Christians from certain churches in China also disapproved of the term. In general, fundamentalists and some evangelicals believed that CCs should not be called Christians because they did not wished to be identified with the church and they diverged significantly from the faith of the Christian churches. A more appropriate nomenclature was needed.

As Liu responded to these criticisms, he agreed that the term "Cultural Christian" could cause some confusion. But he pointed out that any Christian should "have an experience of regeneration through faith, and in matters of conduct, take the sacred teachings of Jesus Christ as the qualities for personal existence and character."[10] Unfortunately "only a small number [of CCs] had such a faith-experience of regeneration."[11]

At the same time the concerns, orientation, and expression of their faith make CCs quite different from those of conventional Christians. They also differ from ordinary Christians in their status in society, their cultural and educational training, and their ethical burdens. CCs are Christians who do not identify with any church; they are either not baptized or they have been baptized but are not members of any church or denomination. The doctrinal beliefs of CCs are also quite different from those held by Christians in churches or denominations.[12] When speaking of the difference between CCs and other Christians, Liu used several contrasts: "Christians" (*Ji du tu*) vs. "Christian religionists" (*Ji du jiao tu*)[13];

"Cultural Christians" (*Wen hua ji du tu*) vs. "ordinary Christians" (*I ban ji du tu*)[14]; "church Christians" (*Jiao hui ji du tu*) vs. "Cultural Christians" (*Wen hua ji du tu*).[15]

Liu further asked why the "Cultural Christian" phenomenon appears in mainland China rather than in Taiwan or Hong Kong? What are the socio-cultural institutions created by this phenomenon?[16] His reply is: "The structure of contemporary daily life in mainland Chinese socialism, combined with the sources of ancient Western thought (i.e., the translation of Christian classics and Western classical writings), together form the socio-intellectual foundation for the phenomenon of 'cultural Christians' in mainland China."[17] Intellectual transformation in Chinese society concomitant with the modernization of Chinese socialism has brought forth all kinds of intellectual questions which are unique to this institutional structure. At the same time, the Chinese Communist cultural policy to absorb ancient "superior cultural heritage," large-scale translation of Marxist writings and classical writings in Western culture, and the availability of twentieth century writings in philosophy, literature, and religion for "internal, restricted reading," all contributed to the importation of humanistic culture (with hidden elements of Christian thought), and provided the primary intellectual source for the "Cultural Christian" phenomenon.

In fact, this type of research in religion is no longer limited to translating books or personal inquiry. Since China opened up her economy, scholarly exchange with the outside world has been stepped up tremendously. For example, Dr. Ping Cheung Lo, a lecturer in religion and philosophy at Hong Kong Baptist University, has referred to his own participation in a summer intensive course on the mainland on religion and culture. The content for this course included materials on Confucianism, Daoism, and Buddhism, but the emphasis was on Christianity.

Among the one hundred and forty in attendance, most were university lecturers, graduate research students, university students, and cultural workers.[18] I, too, have also participated in many similar events in cultural exchange. These included the 1994 conference on "Christian Civilization and Modernization," cosponsored by the Amity Foundation and the Institute for the Study of World Religions of the Chinese Academy of Social Sciences. Also in 1994 the first conference on Chinese and Western Philosophy and the Study of Religion was sponsored by the department of philosophy of Beijing University. Many organizations in China are deeply interested in the unique perspectives which Western Christianity provides on various issues of concern to them. At the same time, as Dr. Li Qiuling, professor of philosophy at the People's University, pointed out: "The Chinese Academy of Social Sciences, various provincial academies of social sciences, and many universities, have established institutes for the study of religion; Beijing University has recently launched a department of religion; under these auspices are many programs for the study of Christianity."[19] Many scholars in the humanities regard Christianity as a social phenomenon which impacts various dimensions of human life; they are currently involved in researching topics which deal with the relationship between their own field of inquiry and the Christian faith. Their open attitude and positive spirit of inquiry are beyond dispute; some of these scholars have even turned to a faith commitment in Christ as a result of their own research, thus becoming "Cultural Christians."

However, Li Qiuling also pointed out that the study of Christianity in China did not begin with the current wave of interest. In the past, in a sort of dogmatic control, mainland Chinese scholars simplified things by pitching Marxism against all other thought systems, with the intent of critiquing and supplanting all others through Marxism. However, since China's opening, scholarly circles went through a journey from critique to a tolerance and search for a common ground. They sought to discover some positive elements from other thought systems in order to enrich themselves or to resolve the current "faith crisis" in China.[20] Therefore there is a new movement of cultural synthesis in the making in China today, along with a phenomenon of cultural pluralism. The "Christianity fever" in China is merely a part of this overall trend; in terms of depth and breadth, and as the study of other religions and output, this interest in Christianity cannot compare with Chinese interest in other thought systems.

All of the above form the immediate context for the emergence of CCs. However, the broader context has to do with the formation and development of the SMSCs. Therefore the first half of this chapter discussed the historical and cultural background of the SMSCs arising out of the social changes in China since 1949. This broader context helps us understand the unique characteristics and the intellectual expression of SMSCs. In short, since 1978, a generation of scholars emerged in China who was engaged in the study of Christianity. It began with the "theory" fields followed by scholars in history, art, literature, and the humanities. They reflected on and critiqued the "leftist" tendencies and the erroneous interpretation of religion of the 1950s, 1960s and 1970s, especially during the Cultural Revolution (1966-1976).

With a scientific spirit of academic inquiry, scholars reassessed the religions of the world, including Christianity. During this process of academic inquiry and personal experience, some of them decided to identify with Jesus Christ in terms of personal response and faith. They grew in their understanding, experience, and interpretation of the Christian classics and Christian theology. With their own research and original writings, they began to promote a "Christian movement" in China. However due to all kinds of

115

considerations and external factors — primarily because of their theological views — they were unwilling to join the Roman Catholic Church or any Protestant denomination. They did not receive baptism and did not participate in the Sacraments. Thus they were regarded as different from ordinary Christians. Yet having had a faith experience in Jesus Christ, CCs were also different from the rest of the SMSCs.

## The Parameters of "Cultural Christians"

When we describe the various phenomena and dimensions of "Cultural Christians," we must emphasize a basic distinctive which has been expounded by Dr. Liu Xiaofeng: " 'Cultural Christians' does not refer to those scholars in China's universities and academic institutions who are engaged in the study of the history and culture of Christianity (that is, SMSCs as defined in this chapter). Rather, they are intellectuals and cultural leaders who have had a personal transforming faith experience. Only those who have trusted in Jesus Christ should be considered Christians. Not every scholar who studies Christianity is a Christian. This should be obvious without saying."[21]

Li Qiuling, in extending Liu Xiaofeng's analysis, divided these SMSCs into three categories according to their personal experiences:

1. The majority of SMSCs seek an objective, neutral study of Christianity as a historical, cultural, and social phenomenon.

2. Then there are those SMSCs who have a positive impression of, or who are sympathetic to Christianity. Li considers himself one of them. Their number is small; their affirmation of Christianity is largely in terms of a spiritual intellectual value system (*Jing shen jia zhi ti xi*). They hope to discover positive elements from this Christian system and integrate them into Chinese culture.

However, the faith systems which they may affirm may not be limited to just Christianity.

3. The very small minority who have exercised faith in Christ. They are academicians and theologians at the same time. Within the entire SMSC community, only these should be called "Cultural Christians." Li Qiuling further identifies Liu Xiaofeng as a representative of this third group.[22]

But since Ping Cheung Lo coined the term "China's Apolloses" one can see that the list of mainland Chinese scholars thus identified has not been limited to the third type of SMSCs.[23] Besides Liu Xiaofeng, Ping Cheung Lo introduced these scholars:

1. He Guang-hu is a researcher in the Institute for the Study of World Religions, Chinese Academy of Social Sciences. He is chief editor of the book series *Zongjiao yu shijie* (Religion and the World) and is an editor of the journal *Ji du jiao ping lun* (Christian Culture Review). He is also a prolific writer in the theory of religion. He is particularly fond of the writings of Paul Tillich and John Macquarrie.

2. Zuo Xin-ping is a member and vice-president of the Institute for the Study of World Religions, Chinese Academy of Social Sciences. He has written and edited many volumes on Christian thought, such as *Ji du jiao wen hua mian mian guan* (Perspectives on Christian Culture), *Sheng jing jian shang* (Appreciating the Bible), *Ni bu er* (Niebuhr), and *Ji du jiao wen hua bai wen* (One Hundred Questions Answered on Christian Culture).

3. Tang Yi is a researcher at the Institute for the Study of World Religions, Chinese Academy of Social Sciences. He has edited *Ji du jiao shi* (A History of Christianity), and has written *Xi fang wen hua yu zhong shi ji shen zhe xue si xiang* (Western Culture and Philosophical and Theological Thought during the Middle Ages).

4. Zhao Dun-hua is a professor and vice-chairman of the philosophy department of Beijing University. His new work is the *Ji du jiao zhe xur i wu ling ling nian* (1500 Years of Christian Philosophy).

Ping Cheung Lo thinks that, through their personal efforts and their astounding prolific publishing record, these mainland Chinese scholars have significantly raised the level of understanding of Western religion among mainland Chinese intellectuals, so much so that they are no longer ignorant about the crucial role Christianity played in Western culture.[24] However, since they have minimal contact with the church and their theological knowledge did not come from the church or the seminary, Lo fears that:

> [T]heir understanding of the Christian faith may be correct, but not adequate. They bury themselves in theological tomes, but seldom read the Bible; they interact with other scholars, but do not have church life. They talk of Christian theology, but are detached from the faith community of Christians. They love theology, but may not love God. God is the object of their study and thought but may not be the object of prayer and worship.[25]

Yet, unless we exclude all SMSCs, including the third group of "Cultural Christians" from the community of believers, the concept of "China's Apolloses" — scholars with a solid background who desire and zealously propagate the Christian faith, but have an incomplete knowledge of the faith-will only create more division and controversy.

The reason for this is that the "Apollos" concept fails to distinguish between the three types of SMSCs. On the one hand, this concept does not do justice to the identity of CCs as those who have believed in Christ (or it implies that their faith is inadequate). On the other hand, it imposes on the first and second type of

SMSCs (those who may be neutral toward Christianity, or who may identify with only certain aspects of the Christian spiritual-intellectual system) a value orientation which they themselves can not accept. Furthermore, there is as yet no consensus among scholars both in and outside the church as to what to make of Apollos in the New Testament. This makes Lo's concept more vague, difficult, and controversial.

## The Distinctives of "Cultural Christians"

According to our observation, CCs share the following common characteristics with ordinary Christians: faith in Jesus Christ and acknowledgment of the Old and New Testament Bible as the basis of faith.

However, the concrete content of these common points requires further explication. For example, what is the nature of their faith in Jesus Christ? Is it a faith in Christ as the symbol and example for an ethical spirit, or faith in Christ as the Creator of the universe who has entered history to redeem people, the world, and the cosmos? When the Bible is accepted as the norm, what is the scope and form of this authority? How are the Bible's teachings on the church and the sacraments received? We believe that it is reasonable and valuable to raise these questions.

Dr. Ka-Lun Leung of the Alliance Bible Seminary in Hong Kong has observed that there is often a methodological truncation among CCs, "especially in handling ideas in theology apart from Biblical studies."[26] Is this approach in interpreting the Christian faith in philosophical terms, without adequate consideration of the Bible's teachings, consistent with a faith in the Old and New Testament as Scripture? Besides, the attitude of CCs toward supernatural elements in the Bible is not clear. They often identify with the cross and a suffering God, but seldom refer to the resurrection of Christ or to his redemption. It is encouraging to know that their beliefs are based *on the Bible*, but this is not sufficient. We must ask: do they base their beliefs on all that the Bible teaches, that is, in its entirety? This is directly related to their understanding of and receptivity to the teachings of the Bible, and their attitude, orientation, and perspective concerning various issues. We are very concerned about this.

Li Qiuling, in his article "The Interaction between Theology and Culture," discussed the relationship between subject and faith.[27] According to Li, the academic world is not obliged or responsible to the church or to the world of theologians. The highest standard for academic research is being scientific; thus, every individual or society has the right to understand the Christian faith from its own perspective, based on its cultural or educational background. Liu Xiaofeng borrowed from Ernst Troeltsch's classification of the forms of Christianity and categorized CCs as "mystics." That is to say, in their institutional form, CCs practice an individualistic faith; in their cultural form, they are creative and activity-oriented; and in their theological reflection, they are oriented toward scientific criticism.[28] We have no major problem with this viewpoint. We also do not object to Li's point that God belongs to all humankind; whether a person is a Christian or not, he has the "right to know his own God."[29] However, we do have the responsibility to clarify this: is the one who is "his own God" still "the God of the Bible?" As Li has pointed out, "Is the Christian faith as understood by mainland Chinese scholars the true Christian faith?"[30]

How are "Cultural Christians" different from ordinary Christians? The difference lies in their journey to faith, their identification with the church, and their relationship to the sacraments.

First, their unique journey to faith. At this moment in history, people in China may come to faith in Christ in several ways:

1. Those who grow up in traditional Christian homes and follow their parents into the Christian faith.

2. Others are influenced by the clergy. They listen to the preaching of priests or ministers, are touched by it, and decide to receive baptism. Whether Roman Catholic or Protestant, there is a formal procedure for joining the government-authorized, open churches. A person may be influenced by friends or relatives, or by their circumstances and experiences. They may gain an insight to the folly of this life and seek a higher value in life. They may be curious about the church but develop a sense of belonging only after they begin attending. They may even go to church in order to seek a more meaningful life beyond their toil and labor (especially in rural areas, where life is simple, and basic cultural and recreational activities are lacking, a good number of adults and youths go to church in order to listen to the music and the preaching). After they begin attending church, and have a desire to join the church, they must apply for membership. The church sends a representative to visit them at home where they are individually scrutinized and evaluated. Then they are scheduled in groups to be baptized, and their names entered on the membership roll.

3. Those who desire to become Christians after listening to gospel radio broadcasts from overseas. This is more common in Guangdong, Fujian, and Zhejiang.

4. Through free lance (or underground) evangelists. There are many who become believers in this way. However there is no normal procedure, the number of believers varies and is unstable, and worship services are not held regularly.

5. Individuals who are baptized by overseas clergy, becoming Christians in a formal manner.

6. Common profession of faith within small groups. Some meeting points in certain locations exhibit this phenomenon. This phenomenon in China is worthy of further study and research. These Christians believe that Jesus Christ did not teach that one can only become a Christian through the church or through clergy (there are many people under this category).

The six types of believers above have one thing in common: they are all recognized as Christians through the church, through clergy, or through a religious group. In other words, there is a third-party intermediary. This is not so with "Cultural Christians." They come to faith in Christ through a gradual process of study and experience of the Christian canon and theological classics, and through their own research into and observation of the history and present state of Christians in China. People in the church who oppose the "Cultural Christian" concept feel that these intellectuals are only affirming their own identity. Therefore CCs are not recognized, accepted, or affirmed by the church. But CCs themselves feel that they have direct fellowship with God; they interact with the Word of God and journey with Christ. Their affirmation is from Jesus Christ; they feel that the church is not necessary as a means of affirming their identity as Christians. In the Bible, the church began to exist only after Jesus left the world.

Second, "Cultural Christians" respect the contemporary Roman Catholic Church and the various Protestant denominations. However, they place themselves outside and above them. They view the church as a historical-social product. The church was formed because "the early Christians were brutally oppressed by the political power and must band together."[31] In the West, the division of the church into denominations was a result of political forces. "The various denominations within Christianity are historical categories of the Christian religion, and not ideal categories."[32] Moreover in China, the history of Protestant missions has been viewed as intricately related to the aggression against China by imperialist powers. As soon as the Protestant missionaries arrived in China they began to develop their own spheres of power respectively. Several hundred mission societies are represented in *The Christian Occupation of China* (1923), a volume which listed the work of mission societies in each provincial capital. For example, six denominations placed missionaries in Zhejiang Province from 1842 to 1911. Later three more denominations entered, including the Presbyterian Church of the United States (South). This led to the need for denominations to come into comity agreements so that they could divide their forces according to spheres of activity. These developments gave a very negative impression to Chinese intellectuals who otherwise desired to learn more about Christianity. After 1955 the Protestants were united in China; this unity remained intact as late as the 1980s. However, due to the past influence of denominations, some searched for their old roots, and in effect intervened in the church in China. Thus in some places there was division or interdenominational conflict; this turned "Cultural Christians" away from the church.

Since the church is not operating at an ideal level of competency, and the institutional church is still an official government agency, "the ability to do pastoral work is weak, and the messages preached are irrelevant," says doctoral candidate Zhang Xian-yong at the University of Basel, Switzerland.[33] Since the registered church is regulated by the government and the "Three-Self" program is becoming increasingly irrelevant to the present reality, the spiritual thirst of these mainland Chinese intellectuals cannot be quenched. Add to this the fact that the phenomenon of "Cultural Christians" did not appear as a result of church or missionary activities, and that some of these scholars have been rejected by church circles in mainland China, it is understandable why they do not want to get involved.

Furthermore, there are very pragmatic considerations in the political and academic contexts. We can understand why the majority of these scholars in China have not joined the organized church. At the same time we must understand that they have rebelled against a monolithic and authoritarian atheism, and have come into contact with "the death of God" and Western theology against a background of the erosion of the authority of the church. This is how they turned to Christ. Bo Fan, editor for the Social Science Documents Press of the Chinese Academy of Social Sciences, spoke on behalf of many Chinese intellectuals:

> Their unique individual experiences make them wary of any 'truth' which has been universally recognized since the May Fourth Movement. At the same time they are wary of the nihilistic thought and temperament in both traditional and modern China; this is akin to the post-Auschwitz skepticism toward the orthodox church and theology, and toward nihilistic philosophy. They came out of the various kinds of 'we,' and became the reflective 'I.' ... And the meaning of the church (the way, the truth, and the life) has reference to 'I' and 'I believe,' and not to the 'we' and 'we believe' bonded by the church.[34]

All of the above factors make it no surprise that "Cultural Christians" have real reservations about the organized church and about becoming "church Christians" (*jiao hui ji du tu*).

But after we have adequately understood and empathized with their concrete situation, we need to point out that some are deficient in their understanding of the church, because although they have believed in Christ, they have not clearly seen where Christ is present today. They have not understood that the risen Christ has built the church as His own body by the power of His Spirit. They seemed to have confounded the community of the church, formed out of that new, ontological relationship which humanity enters into through receiving Jesus Christ, with the denominations which arose out of subsequent history. Therefore we must stress anew that the place of the church is not so negative in the Bible. In the Bible, the church has at least a fourfold meaning:

1. The church is the people of God (I Peter 2:9; Hebrews 12:18-29; 1 Corinthians 3:16-17; 6:19; II Corinthians 6:16).

2. The church is the Messianic community (Luke 2:11; 4:21; 11:20; 12:32; Matthew 16:18; 18:18).

3. The church is the Body of Christ (Ephesians 1:22-23; 2:16; Romans 8:9-11).

4. The church is the fellowship of the Holy Spirit (John 14:18; 16:12-14; Acts 5:32; 13:2; Romans 5-8; Galatians 4; II Corinthians 3:17; Galatians 5:22).

On this foundation, the church may be understood differently:

1. The church invisible vs. the church visible.

2. The church local (congregation or parish) vs. the church universal (the people of God).

3. The church as organism vs. the church as organization.

And the marks which distinguish a church should be:

1. The proclamation of the Word of God.

2. The administration of the Sacraments — baptism and the Lord's Supper (these two are received both by the Roman Catholic Church and by Protestants).

3. The administration of discipline, including administration and sanctions (I Timothy 5:20; Matthew 18:15-18; I Corinthians 11:27; II Thessalonians 3:6-15; I Corinthians 5:5, 11; Galatians 1:9).

Thus it is very hard for us to imagine how a Christian can be completely detached from the life of the church, and at the same time be completely true to the teaching of the Bible on the church. There we hold that the distinction between a "Christian-believer" (*Ji du xin tu*) and a "Christian-religionist" (*Ji du jiao tu*) is only a superficial one; there is in reality no ground for it. As Christian thought continues to be propagated and received among mainland Chinese intellectuals, we can expect that a larger number of intellectuals will believe in Christ and become "Cultural Christians." But if they continue to wander outside the church or reject the church, a very serious problem will arise. This issue deserves reflection and corrective measures by both CCs and by the church. This prompts us to understand a third distinctive which sets CCs apart from ordinary Christians.

Third, most "Cultural Christians" have not received baptism. According to Liu Xiaofeng, "in terms of church membership, the distinctive meaning of 'Cultural Christians' is that they are Christians without church membership, have not received baptism, or do not belong to any church or denomination."[35] But a Christian who confesses faith in the Bible would not easily forfeit the Great Commission issued by the Lord Jesus Christ after his resurrection (Matthew 28:20). It is obvious that baptism is necessary, but for some CCs baptism is merely a ceremony which symbolizes a person's change of heart to live a clean life; there is no inherent meaning to the sacrament. In addition, since divergent interpretations of baptism in church history have given rise to denominations such as the Baptists and the Anabaptists, this encourages CCs to think that baptism is a dispensable ritual in the church.

At this point, we should try to understand some of the contextual factors which explain why some of the "Cultural Christians" have not been baptized. Due to all kinds of external limitations and difficulties, it is quite understandable that when a person becomes a Christian, he or she does not receive baptism and join the church. There is precedent for this in a similar situation before the disintegration of the Eastern European bloc. However, this does not mean that we have sufficient ground to doctrinally reduce the sacraments of the church, baptism and the Lord's Supper, into a dispensable, nonessential ceremony. According to the Bible's teaching, especially the Apostles' teaching, baptism signifies:

1. Uniting with the Lord, to "put on Christ" (Galatians 3:27), especially:

   A. Uniting with the redemptive act of the Lord, to die with Him, and to rise with Him (Romans 6:1-5; Colossians 2:11-12), taking part in God's new creation (II Corinthians 5:17), and sharing in His glory in the new heavens and the new hearth (Colossians 3:1-4).

   B. Uniting with the body of the Lord, that is the church (Galatians 3:26-28; I Corinthians 12:12-13).

2. Baptism signifies entrance into God's kingdom and life under God's sovereign rule (John 3:5; Matthew 12:28; John 12:31-32; Romans 14:17; Colossians 1:1-14).

3. Baptism signifies the transformation from death to life and the commencement of a life lived in obedience to the law of God (Romans 6:4).

Yet baptism and the Lord's Supper complement one another; one can not have one without having the other. This is because baptism is effective with one administration; it is the beginning of the Christian life. The Lord's Supper, however, is a recurring sacrament to be received as a Christian grows in the body of Christ. Therefore baptism can be seen as the necessary prerequisite for the Lord's Supper (Acts 2:3 8, 41-42), while the Lord's Supper is the confirmation of baptism. Both are administered in the corporate life of the church. Therefore, when CCs, for whatever reason, fail to participate in the sacraments of the church, there is a significant loss in the life of the Christian. This loss may be necessary, but it is regrettable.

One reason why CCs put little significance on the church and the sacraments is that they regard the Christian religion as a tradition born within the Western cultural context; the church, sacraments, or even the Bible, are all merely a part of this cultural tradition. Since they have an anti-traditional bent in their background, CCs regard the church and the sacraments as dispensable. This anti-traditional stance is also seen in what Ka-lun Leung calls "truncation in the pulse of thought." Leung points out that, as they write about other theologians in their academic writings, CCs tend to "understand and interpret their specific concepts and ideas in isolation, and rather arbitrarily compare these with the concepts of other theologians, without due regard to the fact that the two theologians actually belong to very different theological traditions."[36] This, to some extent, illustrates their lack of respect to tradition.

We firmly believe that the Bible and tradition is inseparable; there is an extremely important relationship between the two. In a narrower sense, tradition refers to all church customs outside the Bible, or even contrary to the Bible. In a broader sense, tradition is the accumulation of the Christian faith generation after generation, including the orthodox Christian faith within the Bible and without. This "tradition" in the broader sense includes not only theological thought, but also the sacraments, worship, and other symbols and rituals. Each community, no matter how loose institutionally, will not fail to have its own tradition. As the second century Church Father Irenaeus defended the Christian faith against the so-called "Christian" heresy, Gnosticism, he pointed out the relationship between Scripture, church, and tradition. Irenaeus established the church's orthodox position because he, and the believers of whom he was the head, confessed that they abided with the teachings of the Apostles (Scripture), which were publicly transmitted (tradition) in the community established by the Apostles (church). In other words, in the early Christian community, church, tradition, and the content of biblical proclamation were one (this is called the "coincidence view").

In the Middle Ages, the teachings of the church and of church tradition often went beyond Scripture. At first, the motives for certain traditions were understandable: they sought to supplement Scripture where Scripture was not clear (this was called the "supplement view"). Later, however, the church authorized certain traditional teachings outside the Bible as equal in authority with the Bible. This led to the protests of the Reformers in the sixteenth century. The Protestant Reformers merely insisted that the Bible should have a higher authority than the church or tradition. They did not despise tradition; they wanted to affirm that all church controversies be adjudicated by the Bible. The Roman Catholic Church, from the Council of Trent (1546) to the Second Vatican Council in the 1960s has always insisted in the church's final authority to interpret Scripture and tradition. Protestants, however, hold on to Scripture's final authority above church and tradition; Scripture also provides the norms for evaluating church and tradition. Thus China's "Cultural Christians" should also believe in Scripture in its entirety (II Timothy 3:16), as well as in Scripture's teaching concerning the church and the Sacraments. These are not merely traditional beliefs of Western faith-communities; they are the timeless teachings of Scripture which are not open to revision. These are norms which "ordinary" or "traditional" Christians, as well as "non-traditional" or "Cultural Christians" must submit to.

## Reflections: An Evaluation of the "Cultural Christian" Phenomenon

We agree that the "Cultural Christian" is not a phenomenon unique to China; their numbers and impact may not be as great as some optimists within the church may think. However, compared with the "fever" of interest in other religions, the surge of enthusiasm in various academic circles, and the numerical growth of Christians in China, we can only say that this "Christianity fever" is a relatively positive situation. It is largely a cultural development. In any case, their growth in China is an encouraging sign. We believe that, whether in terms of culture or theology, CCs are highly significant and will exert a long-term impact.

In terms of theology, we must admit that the Chinese church (including the church in mainland China and among overseas Chinese) is rather narrow-minded. The narrowness of the overseas Chinese church consists of its limitation to the ecclesiastical and theological traditions inherited from the West. The church in mainland China, on the other hand, is limited by the contradistinction between the registered church and the house church communities. The registered churches follow the "Three Self" platform under the leadership of the state; the house churches take on characteristics of folk religion. The tensions between the two and the limitations therefrom are obvious. These limitations result in the failure of Chinese theology to truly reflect China's own traditions, culture, and contemporary context. The issues which the Chinese church reflects on are largely Western issues. Chinese theology has been highly irrelevant to Chinese traditional culture or the contemporary context. On the other hand, since the "Three Self" churches seek to "express the harmony with the authorities of the state,"[37] they express the Christian faith in terms of an extreme version of the historic, rationalist, liberal school of theology. Over against this, the house churches have strenuously denied the meaning of history and culture for the Christian faith. They espouse an extreme form of fundamentalism which is highly intolerant and they have sacrificed the openness of the Christian faith. "Cultural Christians" are situated between these two polarities. If they can hold onto a biblical faith and can engage in theological reflection in the Chinese cultural context, they have the potential to reconcile between these two extremes and to forestall any crisis they may bring upon the church. This is our expectation concerning "Cultural Christians."

On a more concrete practical level SMSCs and CCs have brought the newest currents of theological thought into the Chinese church. They will create a definite impact on the rather bland theological scene in the Chinese church. In a new competitive situation, they will prompt theological educators (or even the whole church) to re-prioritize their work, to produce more writings with depth. The Chinese theological scene will become more vibrant and will renew itself through discussion and interaction. This should be a blessing to the Chinese church. These new elements should stimulate the Chinese church to re-evaluate the scope of her vision (for example, her mission among intellectuals and to the world of culture), and help re-define the place of theology (including the re-evaluation of denominational mentality and theology). The church would be encouraged to make a more positive response to mainland China, and to make herself attractive to the Chinese people in other parts of the world. We do not take the position that the "Cultural Christian" phenomenon constitutes a crisis for the Chinese church. We believe that this challenging phenomenon should be understood as a unique opportunity for the Chinese church at the dawn of a new millennium. At the same time "Cultural Christians" should earn their right to play a significant role in the life of the church in China.

From the point of view of culture, CCs have the potential to help change the place of Christian thought in China's cultural-academic circles, via the introduction of Christian thought to the Chinese masses through research and translation. As Li Qiuling said, "starting from the stratosphere of culture," a "comprehensive understanding of the Christian faith" can help the Chinese people to "experience faith in a broader context."[38]

We must concede at this point that the church in China and the overseas Chinese church, has taken a very conservative, or even skeptical, posture toward the relationship between the gospel and culture. This is an imbalance. As the Willowbank Report of the Lausanne Committee on World Evangelization pointed out, all theological exposition is affected and limited by its cultural context.[39] Richard Niebuhr delineated five relationships in *Christ and Culture*: (1) Christianity against culture, (2) Christianity in culture, (3) Christianity above culture, (4) Christianity and culture in paradox, and (5) Christianity transforming culture.[40] With the exception of the first model, the other four all point to some measure of tolerance toward culture on the part of the gospel or of theology. Therefore, if we can take hold of the present opportunity and understand that the emergence of the "Cultural Christian" phenomenon is a sign that China's intellectuals are seeking direction for Chinese culture, and if we can offer proposals which have a solid theoretical foundation and which can truly shape the future, we will be able to:

1. Contribute to the transformation of Christianity from its present marginal place in Chinese culture, society, and academic circles.

2. Contribute to changing the traditional confrontational relationship between Christianity and Chinese culture.

3. Make a real difference in China's social structure and thought, and help bring about renewal in Chinese culture, which is undergoing rapid change at the present.

At the same time, we will contribute toward the development of Christianity in China. We must understand the background, life-context, academic, and theological training of the "Cultural Christians," the limitations these imposed on them, their keen pursuit of the indigenization and contextualization of Christianity in China, and the integration of culture into theology. We must also understand that they are not like some Christian scholars who can still "breathe the air" of Christianity while functioning outside church circles. Therefore, at this embryonic stage, there will be a greater likelihood of imbalance and confusion in the doctrinal and theological understanding of China's CCs and their efforts to integrate culture into theology.

Therefore, Christians outside the church should be keenly interested in the thought and writings of "Cultural Christians," and in a spirit of learning together and from each other, offer timely reviews and revisions to some of their views. Or Christians can point to the views on a particular issue, taken by the historic church, so that China's masses, Christians inside the church, and these intellectuals, can all gain a true and comprehensive understanding and interpretation of the Christian faith.

More importantly, Chinese Christians ought to be encouraged by the fact of the incarnation of God the Son Jesus Christ, which shows that the Word of God has not lost its character because of a particular cultural context. If we can hold fast to the teaching of the Bible as a whole and take the Bible as our highest norm, we can effect an encounter between the gospel and Chinese culture without losing the entire essence of the gospel.

All theologizing should take the teachings of the Bible as the highest norm (even though we do not deny that the Bible itself was written against a particular cultural background). But the value of theology lies in its usefulness in and to a particular culture. The influence of the Christian tradition in Western culture is a well-known fact. In the realm of Chinese culture, theology must dialogue with culture; this is also inescapable. The "Cultural Christian" phenomenon has a very positive significance, from the more profound perspective of Christianity's dialogue with Chinese culture.

Notes

[1] Liu Xiaofeng, *"Han si kun he 'pu shi shen xue' "* (Hans Küng and 'Ecumenical Theology), *Du Shu*, 9 (1988): 77.

[2] Liu Xiaofeng, *"Can yu shang di di tong ku-ji nian peng huo fei er"* (Participating in the Pain of God–In Remembrance of Bonhoeffer), *Du Shu*, 2 (1989): 122.

[3] Liu Xiaofeng, *"Ling ting yu ao mi"* (Hearkening and Mystery), *Du Shu, 3* (1989): 111.

[4] Ibid., 118.

[5] Idem.

[6] Liu Xiaofeng, *"Xin yang di zhong fu yu shang di zhi ai"* (The Burden of Faith and the Love of God), *Zou xiang shi zi jia shang di zhen li* (The Truth which Moves toward the Cross) (Hong Kong: Joint [*San lian*] Publishers, 1990), 195.

[7] Idem.

[8] Liu Xiaofeng, *"Xian dai yu jing zhong di han yu ji du shen xue"* (Chinese Christian Theology in the Contemporary Linguistic Context), *Dao Feng* (Logos and Pneuma), Issue 2, 40, footnote.

[9] Tan Xing, *"Guan yu dang dai zhong guo da lu 'wen hua' ji du tu di shen xue ping zhu"* (On the Theological Reviews of Contemporary Mainland Chinese 'Cultural' Christians), in *Ding* (Tripod), 6 (1990). Tan considers these scholars to be only lovers of "Christian culture." Luo Wei-hong also opposes this concept in his article, *"Shang hai zong jiao shi nian fa zhan chu"* (Tentative Proposals on the Ten-year Development of Religion in Shanghai), *Dang dai zong jiao yan jiu* (Contemporary Religious Studies), 1 (1992).

[10] Liu Xiaofeng, *"Zhei dai ren di he ai"* (The Fear and Love of this Our Generation), *Xiang gang zuo yue* (Excellence Hong Kong) (1993): 113.

[11] Idem.

[12] Liu Xiaofeng, "Chinese Christian Theology in the Contemporary Linguistic Context," 25-26.

[13] Liu Xiaofeng, "The Fear and Love of this Our Generation."

[14] Liu Xiaofeng, "Chinese Christian Theology in the Contemporary Linguistic Context," 25.

[15] Ibid., 27.

[16] Ibid., 28.

[17] Ibid., 30.

[18] Ping Cheung Lo (Luo Bing-xiang), *"Zhong guo a po luo yu xiang gang shen xue jie zhi jiu qi wei ji [shang]"* (China's Apolloses and the 1997 Crisis in Hong Kong Theology, Part 1), *Shi dai lun tan* (Christian Times), Issue 419 (September 10, 1995).

[19] Li Qiuling, *"Shen xue yu wen hua di hu dong [er]"* (The Interaction between Theology and Culture, Part 2), *Shi dai lun tan* (Christian Times), Issue 434 (December 24, 1995).

[20] Li Qiuling, *"Shen xue yu wen hua di hu dong [I]"* (The Interaction between Theology and Culture, Part I), *Shi dai lun tan* (Christian Times), Issue 433 (December 17, 1995).

[21] Liu Xiaofeng, "Chinese Christian Theology in the Contemporary Linguistic Context," 25.

[22] Li Qiuling, "The Interaction between Theology and Culture, Part 2."

[23] Ping Cheung Lo, "China's Apolloses and the 1997 Crisis in Hong Kong Theology, Part 1."

[24] Idem.

[25] Idem.

[26] Ka-lun Leung (Liang Jia-lun), *"You shi wo men qian di zhai ma? [shang]"* (Are We

Debtor Again? Part 1), *Shi dai lun tan* (Christian Times), Issue 421 (September 24, 1995).

[27] Li Qiuling, *"Shen xue yu wen hua di hu dong [san]"* (The Interaction between Theology and Culture, Part 3), *Shi dai lun tan* (Christian Times), Issue 435 (December 31, 1995).

[28] Liu Xiaofeng, "The Fear and Love of this Our Generation," 116.

[29] Li Qiuling, "The Interaction between Theology and Culture, Part 3."

[30] Idem.

[31] Liu Xiaofeng, "Chinese Christian Theology in the Contemporary Linguistic Context," 27.

[32] Idem.

[33] Zhang Xian-yong, *"Quan nei quan wai [shang]"* (Inside and Outside the Circle, Part 1), *Shi dai lun tan* (Christian Times), Issue 439 (January 28, 1996).

[34] Bo Fan, *"Shei di ji du, nei ge chuan tong?"* (Whose Christ, Which Tradition?), *Shi dai lun tan* (Christian Times), Issue 450 (April 13, 1996).

[35] Liu Xiaofeng, "Chinese Christian Theology in the Contemporary Linguistic Context," 26.

[36] Ka-lun Leung, "Are We Debtor Again? Part 1."

[37] Liu Xiaofeng, "The Fear and Love of this Our Generation," 115.

[38] Li Qiuling, "The Interaction between Theology and Culture, Part 3."

[39] *The Willowbank Report: Gospel and Culture*, Lausanne Occasional Papers, No. 2 (Wheaton, IL, 1978).

[40] H. Richard Niebuhr, *Christ and Culture* (New York: Harper and Row, 1951).

# Charting Two Critical Maps for PRC Ministry

*Samuel Ling*

Ten years after Tiananmen Square (1989), the United States-China relations are as unclear and uncertain as ever. The two nations may be headed for a cold war in the field of trade and culture; or with the help of the United States, China may enter the international trade community. In the process, global rules of exchange may be changed. Unfortunately, many Americans, particularly many evangelical Christians, are making China out to be the number one enemy. This is undermining Christians' desire to bless the Chinese people and serve the church in China.

## Time to Re-chart Our Maps

On the other hand, China is responding to this confrontational approach with its own aggressive, anti-American nationalism. A stream of books has been published, such as *The China that Can Say No* (1996), and *Behind the Demonizing of China* (1996). China is accusing the United States of human rights abuse, widespread abortion, and a high crime rate.

If this exchange of hostile rhetoric escalates what will be some of the responses?

- Will Christians from the West serving in China be called back?

- Will Christians from the West serving in Hong Kong be recalled as well?

- Will PRC students and scholars continue to remain in North America in even larger numbers?

- Will PRCs largely become part of the immigrant Chinese community in North America? Or will they continue to seek to mainstream into American society with tremendous effort and creativity?

- Will PRC Christians largely assimilate into the existing Chinese churches in North America? Will the cultural gaps between Taiwan/Hong Kong Christians and PRC Christians be bridged?

- Will the American church's interest in China decrease as the press exposes persecution and abuses in China? Will the manpower, prayer, and love towards PRCs decrease?

- How could this trend be countered with a renewed initiative to reach these strategically placed minds, hearts, and homes?

## Rise of Indigenous PRC Ministries

From this alarming picture enters a new generation of PRC pastors, evangelists, and apologists. This is a fact which American Christians and Chinese churches in North America must accept. Will American Christians and Chinese churches in North America continue with business as usual, aiming directly at PRCs to convert them, or will we recognize the new generation of PRC pastors, evangelists and teachers that have emerged among the PRCs? Not only is there an increase of PRCs being baptized, but there is also an increase of PRC churches and PRC fellowships as well. Will we take a servant's posture and seek to empower, equip, serve, and support them? Will we be like Barnabas — rejoicing, encouraging, and opening doors of opportunities for them? Or will our approach be reminiscent of the period in which missionaries operated in China as "neo-imperialists?" Servanthood or neo-imperialism — the choice is obvious.

## Entry of New Churches and Agencies in PRC Ministry

Not only are PRC pastors and evangelists emerging. An increasing number of churches and mission agencies are entering the PRC ministry field in North America or shifting their focus of ministry to care for the spiritual needs of PRCs. We can distinguish several subgroups among these sister-ministries:

1. Recently formed Mandarin congregations in Chinese churches in North America. While the number of PRC-led churches are still small, there are a number of Chinese churches today which have either reorganized their Mandarin worship service (or one of their Mandarin worship services) to target PRCs or have started a brand new worship service to reach PRCs. Since Taiwan/Southeast Asian Chinese Christians speak Mandarin just as PRCs do, starting this new worship service is an effective transition. Some of these churches recognize that the issue is a cultural barrier and not just a linguistic one. Others are not so conscious of the cultural barrier and continue to use "time-proven" methods.

2. Mission agencies that are already serving the Chinese are shifting their focus to meet the needs of PRCs. Some China ministries are moving further from Hong Kong, and PRC ministry has become one of their primary foci of ministry. Some Chinese-run ministries which have multiple functions and foci, have adopted PRC ministry as one of their new priorities.

3. Still others are expanding their existing PRC ministry to attract North America-wide attention and concern.

4. An increasing number of denominational agencies are refocusing their mission interest among the Chinese people by including a home-missions thrust to reach PRCs. Some are calling PRC pastors to plant new churches.

## Time to Take Inventory

In light of these significant changes taking place around us, we need to address two questions: (1) Do we understand who our coworkers are in the PRC ministry field? Can we identify their unique emphases and approaches? (2) Can we discern the pertinent issues in ministry methods and in philosophy/theology which will shape PRC minds and ministries in the twenty-first century?

## Charting the Map of PRC Ministries in North America

The borders of PRC ministries in North America are not well defined. First, PRCs who are flocking into Chinese churches in large numbers are also leaving the church at the same rate. The leaders of Chinese churches in North America have traditionally come from Taiwan, Hong Kong, or Southeast Asia. The PRCs are forming the majority of church growth in Mandarin-speaking Chinese congregations. As Chinese churches look to future growth, the logical thing to do is to reach and disciple PRCs.

Second, PRC ministry has a natural affinity with China ministries in the West. Many people, such as former *Time* Magazine writer David Aikman, believe that reaching PRCs is a strategic way to reach China and to serve the church in China.

Third, PRCs form one of the largest nationality groups who respond to invitations to international student ministry events such as retreats, conferences, sightseeing trips, and other activities.

All of these make the borders of PRC ministry harder to define. This is probably a gift from God's providence. God is calling (1) the Chinese churches, (2) international student ministries and other home mission agencies, and (3) China ministry groups to work together.

One might identify eight types of ministries in this "larger family" of China/PRC ministries, according to their function.

## Direct Ministries

The pioneers in PRC ministry in the early 1980s are mostly of this type. These are groups which aim to befriend, evangelize, and disciple PRCs. They include:

1. Traditional American campus ministries (e.g. InterVarsity, Navigators, and Campus Crusade).

2. International student ministry organizations (e.g. International Ministries Fellowship, International Students, Inc., and InterFace).

3. Ministries launched by overseas Chinese Christian leaders specializing in PRC ministry (e.g. Ambassadors for Christ).

4. Foreign mission agencies who are meeting the needs of PRCs in North America (e.g. OMF International).

5. Ministries exclusively targeting PRCs (e.g. China Outreach Ministries).

6. Denominational outreach to international students (e.g. Southern Baptists and Presbyterian Church in America).

7. Local churches or local ministries with international students outreach.

8. Individuals and families.

It has been my joy to travel and to encourage American Christians to persevere in sowing the seeds of the gospel. My message to them is: keep up what you are doing — praying, loving, reaching, serving, and giving. This, I believe, represents the most precious spiritual treasure of the American people — generosity, love, and reaching out — which is a scarce resource in world civilization today. Generosity (especially among Christians) is part and parcel of the "spiritual heartland" of North American civilization. We lose a lot — indeed, humanity loses out — if we give up this beautiful tradition, which hails from the Puritan and Great Awakening days. Let us not become weary of doing good (I Corinthians 15:58).

## Direct Ministries-Indigenous PRC Bodies

Some of the new generations of PRC Christian leaders are pastoring churches (e.g. Vancouver, BC; Los Angeles; Albuquerque, NM; Rockville/Bethesda, MD). Some have started their own fellowship groups (e.g. New York). Others have joined existing organizations to reach PRCs (e.g. Los Angeles; Fairfax, VA; Paradise, PA; Athens, OH; Raleigh, NC; Pasadena, CA). Still others have launched new ministries to serve PRCs (e.g. Deerfield, IL).

## Resources-Literature and Periodicals

Chinese Christians and missionaries to the Chinese people have long recognized the strategic importance of literature as a tool for evangelism and discipleship. The most outstanding member of the PRC community is *Overseas Campus* Magazine. In addition to circulating tens of thousands of copies per issue, *Overseas Campus* is also read on the Internet by thousands of PRCs. The magazine has a distinct literary flavor, seeking to influence PRCs with articles which speak from the heart. This represents the strong influence of a literary tradition which dates back to ancient China.

An indigenous PRC attempt to nurture PRC Christians is *Christian Life Quarterly*, launched by Zhijun and Esther Wang in March 1997.

OMF International and Christian Communications Inc. (Hong Kong) have been pioneers in producing apologetic publications for PRCs. Several other mission agencies are producing Bibles and Bible study materials for China which meet a real demand among PRCs in North America.

One of the most innovative resource ministries serving PRCs is the formation of the Chinese Christian Internet Mission in August 1996. Rev. John Tan is a "pastor on-line" proclaiming the gospel and providing pastoral care for PRCs and other Chinese students.

Just about all PRC ministry coworkers agree that PRC ministry needs more relevant, clear, and life-changing Bible study materials.

## Training for PRC Christians and Christian Leaders

Since the late 1980s a number of evangelistic retreats have been held to disciple new PRC converts. In the past two years retreats and "schools" have been started to train PRC Christian leaders.

In December 1996 the Great Commission Center (Rev. Thomas Wang), in cooperation with *Overseas Campus* Magazine (Rev. Edwin Su), China Ministries International (Rev. Jonathan Chao), and other various agencies, launched the School of Servanthood, a two-week intensive time of training and spiritual renewal. The result was a spiritual high point of commitment for many PRC Christian leaders. This event also led to the formation of the Mainland Chinese Ministries Council.

In November 1996 China Horizon (through Zhijun and Esther Wang), in cooperation with Ambassadors for Christ, China Outreach Ministries, and Stephen Tong Evangelistic Ministries International, sponsored a retreat for PRC leaders. The result was the formation of a network of PRC ministers. The subsequent meeting, held July 1-5, 1997 in Fairfax, VA, provided an opportunity for fellowship between overseas Chinese Christian leaders and agencies, and PRC Christian leaders.

In June 1996, Stephen Tong Evangelistic Ministries International (STEMI) launched the Reformed Institute for Christianity and the Twenty-first Century, in order to equip Chinese Christians to respond to the spiritual and intellectual challenges of the twenty-first century. Over one hundred students attended part or all of the four week series. Among the participants were a significant contingent of PRCs. STEMI continues to hold its Reformed Institute in Washington D.C. annually. In addition to the U.S. institutes, other similar seminars are being conducted by STEMI in other parts of the world (e.g. Singapore).

The Chinese Studies Program at Regent College (Vancouver, BC) seeks to train PRCs from China and North America to think theologically and to dialogue with contemporary mainland Chinese intellectual trends. International Theological Seminary (ITS) in Los Angeles has also attracted a number of PRC students. ITS, launched by Dr. John Kim, is specifically dedicated to the development of third-world church leadership. Current president Dr. Joseph Tong, a graduate of Calvin Theological Seminary and a psychologist, has attracted many third-world students to its on-campus and off-campus programs.

Theological education for PRC Christians continues to be a very needy field. Seminaries in North America which have traditionally attracted Chinese students (e.g. from Taiwan, Hong

Kong, Southeast Asia, as well as North American-born Chinese) have recently admitted PRCs into their programs (e.g. Trinity Evangelical Divinity School, Reformed Theological Seminary, and Alliance Theological Seminary). In fact, some of the PRC students in these schools came from churches in China.

Some organizations are providing mentoring, encouragement, and financial support for PRCs who seek theological training. The oldest group is the Seminary Scholarship Fund Committee, launched in the 1970s by Robert Chang and the late Li Ta-jyh. China Horizon is involved in financially assisting PRC theological students (e.g. Yuan Zhiming, Wang Zhijun, and Esther Wang). The Overseas Chinese Christian Writer's Foundation (Dr. and Mrs. David Louie, Cincinnati, OH) is helping PRCs to publish their autobiographies and theological works.

## Explorations and Dialogue in Thought and Culture

Just as PRCs are keen with many questions about faith, thought, and society *before* conversion, they continue to seek strategies to link their newfound faith with thought and culture (both Chinese and Western) after conversion. The following organizations each have specific and unique approaches to their inquiry.

The Boston Chinese Christian Reading Club, later renamed the Chinese Christian Scholars Association (CCSA), seeks to bring together students of theology and religion in Boston's universities, graduate schools of religion, and seminaries for fellowship and discussion. In cooperation with the Ricci Institute on Chinese-Western History of the University of San Francisco (with gracious efforts by the late Father Ed Malatesta), CCSA helps to host an annual conference on Christianity and religious studies in the Chinese cultural context. Schools in the Boston area represented in CCSA's membership include Harvard Divinity School, Andover

Newton Theological School, Boston University School of Theology, Brandeis University, Weston School of Theology, and Gordon Conwell Divinity School. Cooperative projects are arranged with the *Logos and Pneuma* Journal on Tao Fong Shan, Sha Tin, Hong Kong.

Efforts to dialogue with contemporary mainland Chinese thought include not only the Chinese Studies Program at Regent College (see above), but also *Cultural China*, edited by Dr. Thomas In-sing Leung (Burnaby, BC). This journal is involved in dialogue particularly with the New Confucianists, and encourages cooperative writing ventures with professors from mainland China.

Yuan Zhiming, the most celebrated convert among the PRC democracy movement leaders, not only writes for *Overseas Campus Magazine* but he is also the leader of the "God and China" Project. It is hailed as a Christian response to the Chinese TV program *He shang*(River Elegy) shown in 1988. The project is working at finding common ground between Christian faith and ancient/traditional Chinese thought, Daoism, and Confucianism. Yuan believes that one third of Laozi's *Dao De Jing* makes reference to the sage who is a kind of Messiah figure.

Though most evangelicals in North America have not always been comfortable, confident, and trained in engaging in intellectual discourse with various academic disciplines, the church needs to understand and to respond to the issues raised by these and other PRC intellectuals.

## Networking

Two networks seek to link PRC Christian leaders: the Mainland Chinese Ministries Council, which grew out of the first School of Servanthood held at the Great Commission Center (Texas),

December 1996; and the Mainland Chinese Ministers Meeting, which grew out of a retreat in Chicago in November 1996.

Another valuable resource is the umbrella organization known as the Association of Christian Ministries to Internationals (ACMI). ACMI's Board is made up of seasoned international student ministry leaders. Agencies traditionally involved in international student work (e.g. InterVarsity, Navigators, and Campus Crusade) and from local international student ministries are both cooperating and co-leading this movement.

A small circle of Chinese Christian leaders involved in PRC/China ministry network informally to explore the challenges which the overseas Chinese church faces in light of PRC responsiveness to Christianity after June 1989. While the initial funding came from the Chinese Coordination Center of World Evangelism-USA office, for many years the gathering was coordinated by an agency which refers Christian professionals for service in China. PRCs are often invited to be part of this annual dialogue.

It is hoped that the ACMI community and the overseas Chinese PRC/China ministry leaders might find more opportunities for information exchange and cooperation.

## Educational Services for China

PRC ministry is a natural concern for Christian organizations in North America which provide educational and professional services in China. Because they are engaged in direct dialogue with educators in China year after year, such organizations provide valuable insight for PRC workers in the West. Intellectuals in China and PRCs overseas form one seamless tapestry. They must be understood in its global entirety.

## Equipping Tomorrow's Equippers

Since the body of Christ has invested in and raised up so many eager and gifted people in reaching PRCs, how can their ministries be enhanced? And who is working to ensure that and even larger number of trained workers will be available to meet the needs of the twenty-first century?

## Who will reach PRCs in the twenty-first century?

1. PRC Christian leaders, many of whom have begun ministering in the 1990s.

2. Existing Western ministries in international student outreach.

3. Overseas Chinese churches, which will include a much larger segment of PRC members.

4. Christians in North America who have a heart for China, including mission committee leaders in the local church, Bible college, seminary students and faculty, former and future teachers serving in China, and mission executives in various agencies.

5. Third-world mission-minded Christians, such as Korean Christians.

What do these future servants of PRCs need? Information, insight, networking, prayer, fellowship opportunities, and much encouragement.

Before we leave the topic of classifying PRC ministries, we should raise the issues of (a) quality control in PRC ministry, especially in the area of discipling and mentoring PRC Christian leaders; and (b) integrity in promotion and communication with the Christian public. PRC Christians can make a tremendous impact on the Chinese public in the West. Yet, how do we help a PRC Christian grow without turning him or her into a "celebrity" to his or her detriment? And how do we communicate the latest developments in PRC work without overexposing our PRC brothers and sisters to the detriment of their maturing process? These issues can be addressed more effectively if PRC ministry organizations and leaders consult with each other in a cooperative spirit.

## Charting the Map of Issues in PRC Ministry

What are the intellectual issues which PRC Christians wrestle with? What practical as well as theoretical issues emerge in the course of PRC ministry?

### Evangelism and Discipleship Methods

There are many overseas Chinese Christians from Taiwan, Hong Kong, and Southeast Asia who believe that large-scale evangelistic meetings are a crucial part of evangelism. God has raised up powerful preachers since the days of John Sung, Watchman Nee, and Wang Mingdao of the 1930s. Today, evangelists like Stephen Tong, a theologian, apologist, revivalist, and evangelist all rolled into one, continue to conduct crusades around the world.

Evangelistic and revival meetings meet a felt need in many PRCs' hearts because they look for "climax" or "crisis" experiences. The effectiveness of crusades, to a large extent, depends on the pre-evangelistic friendship cultivated, and the follow-up work and assimilation of converts into local churches. It seems that PRCs also benefit from "deeper life" (*pei ling*) meetings and conferences to renew their faith.

Many Americans look upon these evangelistic and revival meetings and wonder whether there are indigenous methods to reach and disciple the Chinese. If by "indigenous" we mean "in

149

harmony with the fundamental worldview of Confucianism, Daoism, Buddhism, and Chinese Marxism," then the answer may be in the negative. However, if by "indigenous" we mean "effective in the experience of the Chinese church throughout her history," then many of these techniques have been used among the Chinese people with *positive* results.

Mainstream American ministries targeting PRCs are mostly very sensitive to the cultural issue. They often ask: What is the most culturally appropriate way to present the gospel? What are the most culturally appropriate ways to disciple PRC Christians? Into this discussion enter seasoned PRC ministry workers who are writing papers and doctoral theses on the topic (e.g. Katie Rawson, Fuller Theological Seminary; and Bruce McDowell, Westminster Theological Seminary). PRC ministry is becoming a subfield within missiology! It is hoped that more Chinese Christians (both PRCs and overseas Chinese) would seriously study evangelistic and discipleship methods.

## The Resurgence of Traditional Chinese Thought

Beyond consideration of methods in evangelism and discipleship, one must ask: What are the philosophical, social science, and theological issues which affect the thinking of the PRCs today? What questions do PRC seekers ask? What values are PRC converts affected by? What do they read and what issues do they think about?

We begin by acknowledging that, as soon as we seek to answer these questions, we are dealing with two larger questions: (a) What are the philosophical and theological issues which Chinese Christians reflect and debate about? This points us to the writings of mainland and overseas Chinese Christian publications, including those coming from Canada, United States, Hong Kong, Taiwan, and mainland China. PRCs read and respond to these books and periodicals, and the output is tremendous. (b) What are the philosophical and social science issues which come from the discussion in the community of mainland Chinese intellectuals at large, both in China and overseas? Which non-Christian issues affect PRC Christians most significantly?

One set of issues stem from a reconsideration of traditional Chinese thought, particularly Confucianism and Daoism.

Dr. Thomas In-sing Leung is one of a small number of overseas Chinese Christians who has been trained by the masters of the New Confucianism (not to be confused with the Neo-Confucianism of the Sung and Ming Periods in traditional China). The New Confucianists in the twentieth century seek the revival of Confucianist thought for the modern world. There are several generations of New Confucianists, the most recent being led by people like Dr. Tu Wei-ming who seeks to make Confucian values relevant to the post-modern information world. Dr. Leung, through his journal *Cultural China*, has created a forum for dialogue between the New Confucianists and Chinese Christians. Being a philosopher rather than a theologian, Dr. Leung's efforts should be regarded as a Christian's attempt to create a presence in the secular field of contemporary Chinese philosophy rather than a theological reflection on contemporary Chinese thought representing a churchly tradition. He enters seriously and sincerely into the themes and methods of contemporary Chinese thought, with all its creativity and risks, including twentieth century social science methods.

Yuan Zhiming was trained as a poet and an author before he became a Christian. In his articles, published both by *Overseas Campus* Magazine and Chinese Christian Mission (Petaluma, CA), he has taken a highly personal approach to the interpretation of the historical faith. Like Leung, Yuan rejects the Western, cognitive, and propositional method of understanding the Christian faith. Such methods do not go deep enough to truly root Christianity in Chinese soil. A poetic, literary, aesthetic, and mystical approach is preferred. For Yuan, the history of Christian thought is also seen as a barrier for a true seeker of Jesus Christ. Yuan's approach would be, "Let us directly knock at the door of Jesus," which echoes Chen Duxiu, editor of the *New Youth* Magazine, on the May Fourth Period (1915-1927). Perhaps one could compare Yuan's approach to Christianity with that of Wu Lei-ch'uan and others of Yanjing University in the 1920s and 1930s (see my book *Xian qu yu guo ke*). Yuan, who is discovering parallels between Daoism and Christian ideas, published *Lao Tzu vs. the Bible* (1997), and is retranslating and reinterpreting the *Dao De Jing* to find a Messiah figure in this classic.

While many missiologists rejoice to see such serious attempts of contextualization by Leung and Yuan, orthodox theologians seeking the doctrinal purity of the visible church on earth may wonder if the spurning of propositional truth will compromise the accurate, competent interpretation and application of God's Word in contemporary Chinese culture. This issue is worth pondering: To what extent should biblical doctrine and evangelical systematic theology speak to the issues of philosophy? Does one have to choose between traditional apologetics (understood to be the defense of the Christian faith and the critique of humanist philosophy) on the one hand, and dialogue (understood by many, incorrectly, to be the neutral pursuit of truth in which Christians and non-Christians participate as equal partners) on the other?

A third major thinker which brings traditional Chinese ideas to bear upon PRCs, is Dr. Ka-lun Leung of Alliance Bible Seminary, Hong Kong. Leung, who writes Chinese church history, has published the history of the Protestant church in Guangdong Province. He treats Chinese church history as *Chinese* history. In response and reaction to what is often perceived as missionary imperialism, Leung takes his cue as a Chinese historian and seeks to carve out the field of Chinese church history as an indigenous enterprise. He has also written several journal articles, outlining the attitudes of Chinese intellectuals toward Christianity, particularly as these ideas relate to patriotism. He has also described how modern Chinese intellectuals since the sixteenth century have given up part of their Confucian tradition in order to adopt Christianity as a newfound faith and value system. In the pages of Hong Kong's *Christian Times* (a weekly newspaper), Leung decries the reappearance of triumphalism in certain China ministries, and takes issue with Dr. Ping Cheung Lo (of the Hong Kong Baptist University's philosophy department) as to the significance of the emergence of "Cultural Christians." We see nationalism and Christianity interacting and integrating in the thought of Ka-lun Leung, reminding one of the tensions between T.C. Chao and Wu Lei-ch'uan of the 1920s and 1930s.

## Modern Man and Ideas

Since the 1970s, Hong Kong's most articulate Christian theologians and social scientists have been writing and speaking on the issue of culture. The Seminar on Gospel and Chinese Culture was sponsored by the Chinese Coordination Centre of World Evangelism in 1985. In the late 1980s Hong Kong Baptist University sponsored several symposia, and today its philosophy and religion departments has a talented team of experts. China Graduate School of Theology's vice-president, Dr. Carver Yu, is a former professor of philosophy at Hong Kong Baptist. These and other schools have contributed much in the area of what it means to be human in the modern world.

The method of contemporary theology has been to focus on the immanence of God at the expense of his transcendence. The intention is to find a God who relates to the pain and agony of modern men and women. Existential philosophy influenced Karl Barth's dialectical method. These themes are found both among theologians of China Graduate School of Theology and PRC centers of research such as *Logos and Pneuma*, the journal edited by Liu Xiaofeng.

The popularity of medieval mysticism in Christian spirituality among Hong Kong's evangelicals is a remarkable development in the 1980s and 1990s. Dr. Milton Wan of Tyndale Seminary (formerly Ontario Theological Seminary), a former lecturer at the China Graduate School of Theology, has taught a number of courses and seminars on the cultivation of spirituality, sometimes understood as Christian sagehood. Chi-Hok Wong, president of the First Evangelical Church Association and the Christians for Social Justice (Los Angeles), is teaching Christians the art of solitude, self-discovery, and intimacy with God. Henri Nouwen's books have been translated into Chinese and published by evangelical publishers in Hong Kong. Asia's Christians, living in hectic, postmodern cities, are exhorted to come away and be silent with God. This fits well with the aesthetic and mystical approach to Christianity of Yuan Zhiming and Thomas In-sing Leung. One can expect the Hong Kong and the PRC theologians of spirituality to converge.

Taking a more traditional, churchly approach, Dr. Edwin Hui of Regent College expounds a trinitarian theology for Christian spirituality in his articles which have appeared in *Chinese Churches Today* and elsewhere.  Hui is an excellent interpreter of the spirituality of James Houston for the Chinese speaking world.

The contemporary search for a Chinese Christian spirituality is a thoroughly modern (or postmodern) phenomenon. It is great to see that traditional Protestant thought is interacting with, and responding to, medieval mysticism in providing more biblical content to Christian meditation.

## *The Influence of Postmodernism*

Before the 1970s, the evangelical theological scene held a

consensus as to God's revelation in Scripture. Propositional truth was received, and the Bible's authority in the areas of science and history, as well as in faith and ethics, went unchallenged. There were disagreements as to precise interpretations of doctrines (e.g. infant vs. adult baptism, predestination vs. free will, covenant theology vs. dispensationalism and the various millennial views on the second coming of Christ).

Since the 1980s, however, the study of language has dominated the field of hermeneutics. We are beginning to see the influence of contemporary linguistics on hermeneutics in the Chinese church. Theological lecturers in Chinese seminaries are expounding postmodern ideas, e.g. that words (signs) are arbitrary, and their meaning uncertain. Both the radical and not-so-radical views of contemporary linguists are presented to the Chinese church, often without critique. (An exception is Wai-Yee Ng's treatment of hermeneutics in China Graduate School of Theology's *CGST Journal*, 1997.)

It is high time that the historic, Protestant emphasis on the sole authority of Scripture and a high view of God, the transcendent sovereign over the entire universe, be heard at large in the Chinese church! One needs to ask: What are my responsibilities as a church leader? To what extent am I obliged to profess the faith of the church of the ages? Am I only responsible to the demands of the academic/publishing community or do I have obligations to the historic, visible church of Jesus Christ as a teacher of the church?

## Theological Influences on PRCs

For the first time, North American graduate students in theology from Taiwan and Hong Kong now sit down at the conference table with PRC counterparts and discuss dozens of topics. For example, the Ricci Institute and the Boston Chinese

155

Christian Scholars Association cosponsored a conference on Christianity and religious studies. Another example is Liu Xiaofeng editing a series called *Contemporary European Religious Thought Series*. In this series are Chinese translations of the works of theological writings from such noted theologians as Karl Rahner, Max Scheler, and Heinrich Ott.

Is the evangelical church in North America and the Chinese church overseas ready to dialogue with, and respond to, this broad-based and profoundly academic interest in religion? Would the Chinese church send statesmen and ambassadors into this academic field of ministry?

## Conclusion

With the rise of PRC Christian leadership, the community of China-concerned Christians has a new partner. Overseas Chinese as well as Western Christians engaging Chinese minds need to rethink our models and theological assumptions. Fundamental paradigms need to be reexamined. I end with a few questions for the reader:

1. Should Western models of evangelism be reexamined? If evangelism is a process, how do we effectively listen to our PRC friends' minds and hearts?

2. Could one justifiably speak of a "Chinese" or "Asian" theology when the Chinese church is turning to the West for cues?

3. At what point does creativity in theology and apologetics become syncretism and heresy?

4. What church models can overseas Christians offer PRC Christian leaders as they develop their own congregational life?

Let us learn from Scripture and from each other in a fresh way so that more PRCs will come to know, love, and serve God.

# Come Join the Family:
## Helping Chinese Scholars in the West Turn to God

*Katie Rawson*

## Introduction and Ministry Context

Mainland Chinese students and scholars (PRCs) have been a fruitful harvest field ever since they began coming to the United States in 1978. But the Tiananmen Square event on June 4, 1989 transformed them from a fruitful field into an even riper harvest almost overnight. Commenting on the June Fourth events, my PRC friends all said essentially the same thing: "Chinese young people are looking for something to believe in. We can no longer believe what the government has told us. So we don't know what to believe or who to trust."

Tiananmen Square placed Chinese students and scholars in a situation of uncertainty about their futures which made culture stress infinitely worse. Afraid of government reprisals for their participation in pro-democracy activities in the United States, they hesitated about returning home.[1] Yet they longed to be reunited with their family members again. Since the identity of a Chinese individual is so wrapped up in his or her reference group, indecision about whether to go back to China put some of them in an emotional "no man's land."

All these factors made PRCs an extremely responsive group during the fall of 1989. Indeed they proved so responsive that the international student ministry that I was leading changed our plans in the middle of the year and began organizing every aspect of our program just to meet their needs. During the winter and spring quarters four Chinese scholars or students committed themselves to Jesus Christ, and at least three were headed in that direction. I interviewed these seven Chinese intellectuals to try to discover some of the factors influencing their turning to God.

The term "intellectual" is used in China to describe anyone with even some college education.[2] Both needed and feared by the government, intellectuals have great potential for widespread influence. Our ministry focused mainly on doctors and scientific researchers over the age of thirty. Because they had prestigious jobs in their home country coupled with their age and family ties, they seemed a little more likely to return to China.

After analyzing significant factors influencing the conversion process for Chinese intellectuals, I contend that Chinese intellectuals come to Christ most easily in the context of a caring community where their emotional, social, and spiritual needs are being met. In this model, an encounter with the power of Christ's love is followed either directly by an allegiance encounter or by a truth encounter leading to allegiance.[3] I will suggest that perhaps the most relevant formulation of the gospel call for Chinese students and scholars is "Come join the family!"

Many of the assumptions I make come from my ministry context. Most of our significant work was done by a twenty-three-member team composed of university students and church volunteers. The team included Christian internationals from Taiwan, Malaysia, India, and Tanzania. In addition to an International Bible Study and dinner, we organized a "Conversation Partners" program which linked American Christians with internationals for weekly English practice and relationship building.

# Influences on the Conversion Process

## *Social Networks*

Social networks are the key factor in the lives of the Chinese. Chinese anthropologist Longji Sun notes this:

> In Chinese culture a man is defined in terms of a bilateral relationship. This relationship is a matter of Sodality....We may say that from birth a Chinese person is enclosed by a network of interpersonal relationships which defines and organizes his existence, which controls his Heart-and-Mind. When a Chinese individual is not under the control of the Heart-and-Mind of others, he will become the most selfish of men and bring chaos both to himself and to those around him. And yet when the definition of his Sodality is extended to the entire community, he is capable of being the most unselfish of men.[4]

The top Chinese leaders were not currently under the control of the Heart and Mind of others, and this brought chaos to the country. The students at Tiananmen Square saw themselves as fighting for the good of the whole country, and they were indeed "among the most unselfish of men."

Being controlled by the group provides security for the Chinese, but it can also be oppressive to them. One response to feeling powerless is to do almost anything to gain power over others. One of my friends said, "Power is everything in China." Coming to the United States does not change the Chinese intellectual's need for a network. They establish kinship-type groups for themselves based on "sameness" — same hometown, same profession, same university, or same mentor.

It is essential to look at individuals in terms of the social networks they are a part of, both here in the United States and at home in China. After doing an analysis of the networks of the Chinese attending one Bible study, Norie Roeder made the following observations:

> [G]aining access to the social network is key for meeting and building new friendships among the mainland Chinese. To be introduced through the network gives one credibility to the Chinese and makes one an insider. Once access is gained, identifying influential members of this network is also key.[5]

Our ministry team identified three influential leaders of networks and invested much time in them. We found that the Bible study grew because key leaders brought more and more members of their networks, and these visitors often continued coming. We also discovered that the networks served as effective "grapevines" for news and gossip and that Christianity was a much-discussed topic when members of the network got together.

The people whom we identified as opinion leaders influenced their networks by inviting newcomers to the Bible study and by bringing up Christianity as a possible solution to China's problems when network members got together to talk. Two of the three opinion leaders were not Christians, but they were suggesting Christianity as an innovation that might help their nation. The third opinion leader was a believer from a Christian family in China. Just before leaving our university for a position on the East Coast, she gave her testimony publicly using an original poem she had written in Chinese. Her influence, coupled with that of the two non-Christians who were considering the faith, helped to make believing in God a viable alternative for network members.

Commenting on the Chinese government's attempts at mass communication after 1949, Francis Hsu and Gordon Chu said:

> All human beings need to receive and give affect....In traditional Chinese culture, the affect was earnestly sought and steadily provided in the context of kinship and kinship-oriented wider social relations....Today these same social networks, permeated with a persistent element of personal affect and buttressed by the residuals of traditional values, form a web of tentacles, as it were, through which the revolutionary message have to pass and become twisted, thus losing much of their original appeal.[6]

Kinship-oriented networks actually worked *against* the communication efforts of the Chinese government. On the other hand, we were able to *use* the networks for communication of the gospel.

PRC intellectuals are also a part of a network of family members, friends, and colleagues at home. This must not be forgotten when we are trying to determine how much "freedom to innovate" the individual has. Some students have privately expressed fear of government reprisals on their family if they make public commitments to Christ in this country. Others have expressed fear of public opinion if they return to China having embraced a "Western" religion.

The parent-child relationship is very strong in China. We have observed that scholars with children seem more concerned with their children's welfare and less concerned about their parents' approval of decisions. Those without children seem to be more concerned with their parents' welfare and/or approval of decisions.

The Christian worker should be careful not to pressure a Chinese student or scholar into making a public decision for Christ without considering the implications for family members. Although letters to and from China were routinely read by government authorities, several of our friends wrote family members about their interest in God. Responses varied from simple non-opposition ("Do what you like") to interest in God on the part of the relatives. Through the years, I have observed Chinese converts lead spouses and/or children to the Lord after families were reunited.

Since in most cases it serves as a kind of substitute family or clan, the Chinese network in the United States seems to exert more influence on the individual than the network in China. There is also considerable variety in the amount of influence the group exerts, reflecting different degrees of acculturation for each individual (Figure 1 shows the various networks in which some of our friends were involved).

## Felt Needs, "Woundedness" and Worldviews

In addition to social networks, the decision-making process of an international student will be influenced by at least three other variables: the circumstances and experiences of the sojourn abroad, the worldview(s) prevalent in the home country, and the worldview(s) of the host country. The circumstances of the sojourn will bring to the fore certain felt needs and may also aggravate or uncover any underlying "woundedness" (need for inner healing) in the individual.

After Tiananmen Square, Chinese students and scholars went through a period of disillusionment and grieving. Any remaining faith they had in their government was shattered. President George Bush's executive order allowing them to stay until 1994 put some of them in a quandary about the future — should they try to immigrate or not? If so, how could families join them?

In the midst of these stressful circumstances, the Chinese needed to know that they were loved (security). They needed

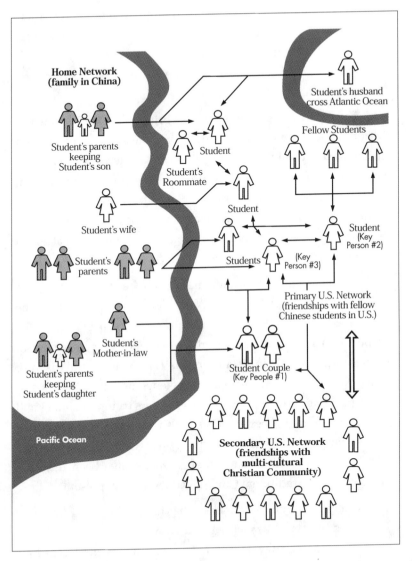

Figure 1

**Social Networks of Chinese Intellectuals in Our Group**

hope for the future, inner peace, and something (or Someone!) to believe in again. There were many things about their circumstances which they could not control, but they were longing for a sense of empowerment and freedom. It is at the point of felt need that the power of Christ's love was demonstrated by Christian communities.

These psychological stresses also bring to the surface any old "woundedness" inside individuals. Shame for acts committed during the Cultural Revolution (1966-1976), bitterness, the need to forgive or be forgiven as a result of things done during that era, and confusion about personal identity are some of the manifestations of woundedness which we observed. As we will note later, these wounds and fear about the future can weaken the wills of those considering Christ.

Felt needs and "woundedness" can be addressed by an encounter with Christ's love. Worldview assumptions must be challenged by Christ's truth as well as his love. It is beyond the scope of this present discussion to describe the worldview of Chinese intellectuals in detail. Francis L.K. Hsu's comparison of traditional Chinese and American societies using postulates and kinship should be of great help to Westerners trying to understand their Chinese friends better.[7] Hsu and Gordon C. Chu have edited a later book which examines changes in Chinese values since 1949.[8] They conclude that although there have been dramatic changes, many traditional Chinese values are still present.[9]

One of my informants stated that his thinking in China was influenced by "scientific method," Marxism, and traditional Chinese (including Confucian) values. All of my informants emphasized the importance of scientific thought to them. Yet traditional Chinese values appeared to have gone underground or reappeared in new forms. The Confucian virtue of loyalty of subject to ruler has been replaced by loyalty of citizen to country. Faithfulness in the parent-child, wife-husband, and friend-friend relationships was still considered the ideal, according to my friends.

The experience of a person with paradigms from two or more worldviews is termed "worldview schizophrenia" by Charles Kraft.[10] In a previous paper I suggested that international students deal with worldview schizophrenia by compartmentalization; they use paradigms from competing worldviews in different sectors of their lives.[11] Thus my Chinese informant mentioned above used paradigms from science and Marxism in his academic and vocational life, but followed traditional Chinese values in his private life. When he began to consider the Christian faith, however, paradigms from all three worldviews came into focus as obstacles in his search for faith.

How did the worldview prevalent in the United States influence Chinese scholars and students since their arrival here? Coming to America only deepened worldview schizophrenia for them. A few paradigms from the worldview prevalent in the United States entered the mix (my informant said 5-10% of his thinking was influenced by American worldview). But my Chinese friends did not seem to be content with compartmentalization as a way of dealing with worldview schizophrenia. *They were looking for a faith which was valid in their scientific pursuits, in their hopes for a democratic China, and in their private lives.* Chinese intellectuals rejected Christianity in the early decades of the twentieth century, precisely because they saw it as a privatized faith with no positive public impact.[12] Figure 2 illustrates the influences on the Chinese intellectual coming from the three sources just discussed.

As noted earlier, the need to believe in something became a significant felt need for Chinese intellectuals after June 4, 1989. So they began to explore Christianity, which many saw as the religion of the United States. This searching is actually not much different from what was happening in China at the same time. Reporting on a visit to China in *World Christian* magazine, Xiao-chun Chen noted a significant change in thinking:

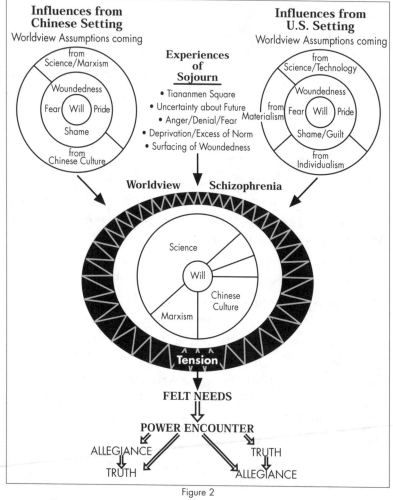

Figure 2

**Influences on the Worldview Change of Chinese Intellectuals**

A remarkable paradigm shift has occurred in the thinking of many Chinese intellectuals. Repeatedly I was told, "I now believe that human nature is evil," or "I no longer believe people to be good." Among the hundreds of Chinese intellectuals with whom I have discussed the nature of human beings, until this trip I had encountered only a handful who would make such a statement.[13]

Chen adds that there is a new interest in Daoism as well as in Christianity. It seems that the post-Tiananmen searching among Chinese intellectuals may be an opportunity for what Anthony Wallace calls "revitalization."[14] Dissatisfaction with the status quo has led to serious reconsideration of major paradigms. The increased spiritual interest among Chinese intellectuals in this country may just be an "overflow" of the spiritual hunger in China.

## Receptor-Oriented Communication of the Gospel

"Receptor-oriented communication" implies communicating directly to the needs of the audience.[15] I asked my informants what would be the best possible news they could read in tomorrow's newspaper. The highest priority for all of them was a new government in China and the second priority was to be reunited with their family members. Given this information, I wrestled with the question, "How is Jesus good news to my friends?"

### The Power of Love

Christ's love answers the felt needs and woundedness described above. All of the informants I interviewed said that the kindness, friendliness, and willingness of Christians to go beyond surface level relationships were what first attracted them to Christianity. Although it may not seem dramatic, the attractiveness of Christians and of the Christian community was, in reality, a power encounter. Unconditional love and listening, coupled with prayer over the long haul can go a long way toward healing some of their woundedness.

Most of our Chinese friends had their own Chinese networks here. Through the weekly International Bible Study meetings and individual "Conversation Partner" meetings, we attempted to become a secondary social network for them. By practicing English with them and sharing practical and cultural information, we helped with the acculturation process.

In choosing to participate in our group, they became part of a process which may be considered conversion through "re-socialization."[16] Our twenty-five to thirty member Bible study was divided into four smaller groups (by gender and English proficiency) for the actual Bible discussions. In these smaller groups we shared prayer requests and answers to prayer and prayed for the needs of group members. Non-Christians were not pressured to share, but they were often happy to have their needs prayed for, even if they said they did not believe in God. Especially for women at least, the smaller groups became significant support groups. (Having a Christian woman from Taiwan present to translate and pray in Chinese made the group times especially meaningful.)

As internationals became a part of the group, I often observed behavioral changes months before an actual verbal commitment to Christ occurred. Jesus Himself said that those who obeyed His teachings would know whether or not his words come from God (John 7:17). *Discipling was actually happening in the context of the group before the person chose to make a public commitment.*

Although I feel that conversion and growth in grace through participation in a Christian group is an appropriate way for

168

international students to come to Christ, there are two dangers. The first is a conversion that is merely sociological or cultural: coming to Christ may be seen as a part of joining the group or as a way of identifying with American culture. The second danger is that of extraction and inappropriate discipling: The converted individual may be discipled in a Western manner (and in English) and be ill prepared for an eventual return to China. I believe that we successfully avoided the first danger by demonstrating unconditional love and refusing to pressure people. The second danger is something with which we wrestled for quite some time.

## The Truth Encounter: Addressing Their Questions

Whereas the power encounter (the experience of being loved unconditionally in a Christian group) was enough to bring some to allegiance to Christ, others needed it to be followed by a process of learning the truth before they would come to the point of commitment. The individuals I interviewed all mentioned belief in the supernatural as a difficulty due to their scientific and Marxist training. I got the sense (and some of them even told me) that intellectual questions were often not the greatest obstacles. The real obstacles, which lay below the worldview level, may be thought of as "will-weakeners."[17] Some of these obstacles were fear of the government or fear of public opinion, confusion about individual identity due to culture shock, woundedness resulting in low self-esteem, and ethnocentrism. Each of these obstacles can be addressed by biblical truth as well as by continued ministry from group members.

The postscript lists some of the implicit (unexpressed) and explicit questions Chinese intellectuals have asked. My informants suggested starting conversations about faith with the relationship between Christianity and the United States' form of government, i.e. the "political meaning of Christianity."[18] Addressing this subject also allowed us to answer implicit questions about a society which facilitates both freedom and security.

One Chinese man said that he loved the Bible study about the "Changed Community" (Acts 2:43-47) most of all the ones we did. Others advised studying texts about Jesus' kindness; still others said that they needed a framework for understanding Jesus' death and resurrection. All of them said that Genesis 1-3 were the most difficult Bible studies we had done. Putting all this information together, I planned a Bible study series which began with a few studies from Matthew on the "Changed Community" and then backed up to look at Jesus changing individuals. By looking at Jesus early on, we would address the deep needs for hope, love, and trust. We then backed up even further to get the historical framework for Jesus' coming before looking at the significance of His death and resurrection. During the following summer, I planned some sessions on the character of God and on apologetics, in order to build up new Christians and provide more truth for those still deciding.

But what about the acknowledgement of sin, confession, and repentance? What exactly does a mainland Chinese person *turn from* when he or she turns to God? Overemphasizing the word "sin" can actually be a stumbling block for the Chinese since the English word "sin" is translated by a Chinese word which means "crime." My informants told me that lying and selfishness were considered wrong in their society. They are also very sensitive to the misuse of power, but by their own standards, many of them were quite good people.

I believe that it is not necessary to have a deep sense of sinfulness or guilt before turning to God — only an awareness of separation from God and a deep desire to be His child. An awareness of sinfulness will develop as a person gets to know God *after* commitment (Hebrews 11:6).

Chinese people turn from unbelief to belief, and from dependence on self or the group to dependence on God and interdependence in His family. "Sin" is best explained as deliberately staying outside of the covenant, and conversion can be viewed as joining the family of God. The parable of the Prodigal Son (more aptly termed the Loving Father) is effective in communicating sin and repentance to the Chinese. Emphasizing the faithful covenant love of God (the Hebrew word is *hesed*, as in Psalm 89:1 and Lamentations 33:22) and pointing out the similarities between this love and the Confucian ideal of faithfulness in certain relationships was quite helpful to our team.

Our network of Chinese friends constantly compared the United States and China, and they were critical of both societies. They were also preoccupied with freedom and power. Given all this information, I prepared Figure 3, a presentation of the biblical alternative to the misuse of power. The covenant community, a setting where individuals are empowered by God and by the group and where power is not misused, is what the Chinese are yearning for. Since so many of their leaders had proved untrustworthy, however, they needed to learn a great deal about God before and as they came to trust Him. In this diagram, "sin" is defined as the worship of power, and Jesus is seen as the One who gives supernatural power to live freely and morally within the limits of covenant (law). This definition of sin should be easily understood. Jesus as the Deliverer who empowers those who feel powerless (as many of the Chinese did at that time) should be very attractive to them.

## *Culturally Appropriate Evangelism*

Receptor-oriented communication also includes the use of appropriate vehicles of communication. One appropriate medium for the prestige-conscious Chinese is *lectures by distinguished*

Figure 3

**The Covenant Community Compared with American Society and Chinese Society**

*professors, scientists, and professional people.* It is helpful if the speaker shares his or her testimony as a part of the lecture, and if question-and-answer sessions are possible. If the speaker is Chinese, the impact may be even greater. *Testimonies* by both Chinese and Americans who speak of Christ's healing power and tell how they came from unbelief to belief can also be quite effective.

Bible discussion groups are generally effective because many Chinese are interested in the Bible and very desirous of practicing English. We addressed the need for English practice by introducing new vocabulary before presenting short segments of videotapes (an apologetic video and the *JESUS* film) and by grouping people according to English level.

Bible discussion groups *can* become boring; they *can* give Chinese intellectuals the impression that we're trying to brainwash them without allowing them to ask questions, and they can resemble the political discussion groups which were required and hated in China. In *Two Years in the Melting Pot*, PRC journalist Zongren Liu devotes an entire chapter to an American Christian's efforts to share Christ with him. Liu was greatly impressed with the American man's wife's ability to "give the right answers" during a Bible study session, but he seems never to have asked a question himself.[19]

We can avoid these pitfalls by trying to make Bible studies fun and interesting. Ministry team members can contextualize parables and act them out with humor; segments from the *JESUS* film or other videos can be used to introduce other studies. Worship songs in Chinese may add relevance and enjoyment to Bible study meetings. Cultural sharing on topics like the meaning of personal names or "What Makes a Hero in My Country" might enliven the smaller discussion groups. An introductory question involving cultural sharing makes a Bible discussion a mutual learning experience and paves the way for discovering how the Bible differs from both American and Chinese cultures.

To encourage people to ask questions that are really on their minds, we may begin discussions with general opinion questions like, "If you could choose your own boss or professor, what kind of person would you choose?" The leader should also deliberately bring up the questions that the Chinese are too polite to ask, even playing the devil's advocate at times. As trust is gradually established, people will become more and more free to express themselves.

Since the Chinese are concrete relational thinkers, anything that is pictorial or visual will help. Stories, parables in particular, have the needed concrete relational character. We routinely used diagrams and simple drawings on a flip chart or overhead projector to reinforce certain points. The flip chart became a helpful means for reviewing Bible history. (An outline of Bible chronology is one of the requests our friends made in the fall of 1989.) For those with limited English, we provided summary sheets and often included a drawing or diagram on the sheet as a reminder of the main points of the study.

Movies and videos by themselves, both Christian and secular, may be used to stimulate good discussions about spiritual things. Taking Chinese friends to Christmas and Easter pageants and other dramas can also be effective. Drama (including opera) has been a popular medium in China for centuries. Bible storybooks with many pictures and even Bible cartoons might be effective. Parris Chang reports that picture storybooks intended for children are popular even among adults in China.[20] Some of our Chinese friends have enjoyed discussing Bible storybooks and C.S. Lewis' *Chronicles of Narnia* in English practice sessions.

## Suggestions for Christian Workers

Much work needs to be done in analyzing worldview change among Chinese intellectuals. My informants were over thirty (except one) and all in scientific fields. Younger students and those studying humanities might have somewhat different worldviews. Much work also remains to be done on the problem of discipling converts who could someday return to be influential both in professional life and in the Christian community.

I do have some recommendations for my colleagues, however. First, when dealing with mainland Chinese (and almost any other international student group!), *target the social network rather than individuals.* Invest yourself and your team in opinion leaders. When a whole group of friends come to Christ at almost the same time, they can work together on deciding how to live out the faith in culturally appropriate ways. International student workers often make the mistake of working with individuals rather than groups.

Secondly, *do not bypass the power encounter and place too much emphasis on the cognitive.* The truth that students are learning needs to be validated by the power of Christian love. *Chinese students are yearning to see a community where hope is possible, and where the individual can have both security and freedom.* God's covenant community is the only place where this is possible, but such a community must be demonstrated to them, not simply discussed in Bible studies. This is why they must be loved (security) but not pressured (freedom) during the decision-making process. This is also why ministry should be done in teams.

Finally, *be receptor-oriented in your communication.* Many older Chinese are not concerned about their lives as individuals, so I do not use Western gospel explanations addressing individuals, even in Chinese translation. J.I. Packer has summarized the content of the gospel in six stories: "God's Purpose," "The Kingdom," "God's People: The Church," "The Grace of Christ," "The Glory of Christ," "God's Image Restored" and "Man's Joy Begun".[21] Most Western gospel presentations communicate the truth in terms of "Man's Joy Begun" or "God's Image Restored." For Chinese, the appropriate story to begin with is "God's People: The Church." Packer summarizes the story in this way:

> In this story the goal of God's action is to have a people who live with him in love.... The gospel call from this standpoint is to accept a share in the life and hope of God's forgiven family by bowing to the Lord whose death redeemed the church and whose risen life sustains it. This is not to put the church in Christ's place, but to preach Christ as the answer, through the church, to every man's problem of isolation and alienation from God and man.[22]

In other words, the gospel call may be given as an invitation to "Come join the family!"

# Postscript:
# The Next Generation

Nine years have passed since "Come Join the Family" was written. Now that we are working with a younger generation of PRCs, some of my thinking about international student ministry has changed.

Like most postmodern young people, the PRC "Generation X" respond well to deep friendships with peers. U.S. friends and conversation partners must make every meeting an experience of mutual sharing and learning and not assume that PRCs will automatically want to listen to what we have to say. For example, I have asked a young Chinese woman with whom I meet to tell me each week everything that seems strange to her about U.S. culture. I receive the gift of learning how we are seen by other eyes. She, in turn, has asked some of the most penetrating questions I've ever heard about the Bible.

Like most of their peers in East Asia, the younger generation of PRCs have worldviews consisting of traditional (Confucian and shamanistic), modern (scientific method, belief in progress and reason) and postmodern assumptions. Shamanistic influences are seen in expecting good luck from God (or good luck charms) and in consulting shamans for healing.[23] Postmodern assumptions include the notion of multiple truths rather than one, knowing through experience rather than reason and an awareness of human misery instead of a belief in progress.[24] At least some PRC young people also share in the postmodern condition; bombarded with media presenting many possible identities, they are not sure of their own identities: they are "de-centered."[25]

Shamanistic assumptions are likely to surface as students get serious about seeking God or after they have made commitments to Christ. Some years ago I was puzzled when a young convert asked me for a picture of Jesus to hang in her car. Then I learned that she had just been in an accident. Confusion over the nature of relationship with God is typical of converts from shamanistic backgrounds. PRCs need to learn early on that relationship with God is a dynamic interaction with a Person, not a contract to guarantee good luck. This understanding is crucial; I have seen backsliding when God did not provide the expected good fortune in a certain matter. As a matter of fact, the two most crucial truths most East Asian students don't seem to easily understand are the character of God as personal and universal, and the dynamic, interactive nature of relationship with God.

Modern influences may be seen in the race to succeed. Many of the younger generation seem more interested in personal goals and less concerned for their nation than the older scholars described above. The race for economic prosperity has dominated China since 1992[26] and the younger students sense a great deal of pressure to "make it" in America.

Postmodern influences show up in the shorter periods of time it seems to take many in the younger generation of PRCs to come to Christ. Although they still ask the most questions of all East Asian students, they seem to have been less deeply influenced by atheistic teaching than the older scholars. Participation in a community offering hope and love is key for them; the community becomes the plausibility structure they need to come to Christ.[27] And like other postmodern young people, the younger PRCs respond to the auditory learning channel; international student fellowships must have worship music which is every bit as contemporary and high quality as that in U.S. student fellowships.

Based on my recent research[28] the following is a list of implicit questions :

1. Is unconditional love really possible? How can I find it?

2. Is there anyone who understands my pain?

3. Where can I find both freedom and security?

4. Where can I find meaning and identity?

5. Is there more to life than making money?

6. What can give me hope for living?


Here is a list of explicit questions and concerns:

1. How could a good God allow so many bad things to happen?

2. I find it hard to believe in God.

3. Aren't there many gods, not just one?

4. Isn't Christianity just a Western religion?

5. Isn't there a conflict between science and the Bible?

6. I find the Bible confusing.

7. People are basically good, but the Bible says they are sinners.

8. Why doesn't God give good luck to good people, especially Christians?

9. How can we believe that the Bible is reliable?

10. How can we believe in miracles (especially the resurrection of Jesus)?

11. Why did God do so many bad things in the Old Testament?

12. How could a good God allow people who have never heard of him to go to hell?

13. I'm not good enough to be a Christian.

14. Aren't Christians weak people?

15. The Bible discusses things which are long ago and far away-how can it be relevant to me?

16. Aren't religious people just trying to use God or the gods to get some good luck?

Core assumptions needed by new believers include:

1. God is personal.

2. God is the creator of the universe, not a territorial god.

3. God wants intimate relationship with human beings and has sent the Holy Spirit to facilitate that relationship.

4. God's love is unconditional — he cannot be bribed or manipulated.

5. The blessing God gives is his presence at all times, not good luck.

6. God also wants us to be in relationship with his people.

7. Jesus Christ is the way to relationship with God, the truth about who God is and the source of real life.

8. "Sin" is refusing, violating relationship with God. "Sins" grow out of this violation.

9. The way to grow is to consistently say "yes" to relationship with God and to relationship with his people. To "repent" is to choose relationship with God and to continue to pursue this relationship, thus continually turning away from the sin nature.

More work needs to be done on explaining sin and the atonement in relational rather than the legal terms preferred by Westerners. The Chinese woman with whom I meet each week was very relieved when I recently explained to her that sin was something more than guilt. Sin is more easily seen by Chinese as the violation of a relationship than as the violation of law. Perhaps the notion of covenant mentioned earlier will be helpful here. C. Norman Kraus has written some insightful material on understanding sin and the atonement in terms of shame as well as guilt.[29]

See Appendices A and B for the diagrams I currently utilize to give an overview of the gospel and suggestions for using these diagrams. Although they conclude with a sinner's prayer, I do not intend them to be used as a "cold turkey" gospel presentation, as the accompanying suggestions make clear.

When PRCs come to Christ in a fellowship led by Caucasians, appropriate discipling and reentry preparation becomes a crucial issue. We Caucasians need to acknowledge that we do not have the cultural understandings needed to disciple Chinese as skillfully as fellow Chinese could. It may seem to us as if we can disciple those students who have assimilated well into U.S. culture, but there are areas of cultural strength and weakness which we are likely to overlook. (Both the receiving and granting of forgiveness seems to be especially difficult for East Asian students, for example. I realized this after thirty-six interviews[30] but wise East Asian Christians know it without having to do research.) And the more discipling Chinese receive in an American fellowship, the more assimilated into American culture they are likely to become. In such circumstances, return to China becomes more difficult and less likely.

Some of the converts in the ministry described earlier joined Chinese churches, and I am glad they did. Our international fellowship helped them grow, but the Chinese church provided the chance to worship in the native language and to work through discipleship issues unique to the Chinese. If new converts hesitate to attend Chinese churches because of cultural and generational differences with their members, perhaps we need to invite members of these Chinese groups to join our fellowships and get to know the young Christians. A great deal of the effectiveness of the ministry described earlier was due to the presence of Christians from Taiwan, Hong Kong and Malaysia on the ministry team.

Some areas where we may be helpful in reentry preparation include teaching new Christians how to feed themselves from the Bible and to lead cell groups. Practice leading and using their gifts in the Body of Christ will be useful if God directs them to house churches. It is crucial that they gain a good understanding of the positive role of trials in the Christian life,[31] something they might not ordinarily get in a U. S. church setting. They also need to learn to listen to God and depend on the Holy Spirit. Developing emotional maturity, character and integrity—not just gaining knowledge—is key for young Chinese Christians. Here again we need to partner with mature Chinese Christians who may be more discerning about these issues than we can be.

With only fifteen percent of PRCs said to be actually returning home, the question of how to facilitate return becomes an issue. I was told by one young Chinese leader that I had no right to make such a suggestion to PRCs since I enjoyed citizenship in the U.S. Yet it is possible to create an atmosphere in a fellowship that encourages members to return home. Groups where students are allowed to lead and use their spiritual gifts and are encouraged to consider how they might "translate" the type of ministry they are doing after arriving home may facilitate serious consideration of reentry. Encouraging and preparing people for reentry seems to be the area of PRC ministry requiring the most prayer and work in the years ahead.

# Appendix A: Resources for Christian Workers

## Books and articles:

Chinn, Lisa Espineli, *Think Home: A Practical Guide for Christian Internationals Preparing to Return Home.* International Students, Inc., 1987.

Chuang, Tsu-Kung, *Ripening Harvest: Mission Strategy for Mainland Chinese Intellectuals in North America.* Paradise, PA: Ambassadors for Christ, 1995.

Hu, Wenzhong and Cornelius L. Grove, *Encountering the Chinese: A Guide for Americans.* Yarmouth, ME: Intercultural Press, 1991.

Jordan, David K., "The Glyphomancy Factor: Observations on Chinese Conversion," in *Conversion to Christianity: Historical and Anthropological Perspectives on a Great Transformation,* ed. Robert W. Hefner. Berkeley, CA: University of CA Press, 1993.

Mirza, Nate, *Home Again: Preparing International Students to Serve Christ in Their Home Country.* Colorado Springs, CO: Navigators, 1993.

Naisbitt, John, *Megatrends Asia: Eight Asian Megatrends That Are Reshaping Our World.* New York: Simon and Schuster, 1996.

Schaumburg, David E., *Manual for Ministry to Internationals.* Springfield, MO: Assemblies of God College Ministries Department, 1987.

Stewart, Edward C. and Milton J. Bennett, *American Cultural Patterns: A Cross-Cultural Perspective.* Revised edition. Yarmouth, ME: Intercultural Press, 1991.

Yum, June Ock, "The Impact of Confucianism on Interpersonal Relationships and Communication Patterns in East Asia," in *Intercultural Communication: A Reader,* 8th edition, eds. L. A. Samovar and R. E. Porter. Belmont, CA: Wadsworth, 1997.

## Sources of Literature and Media

The *JESUS* Film Project
PO Box 72007
San Clemente, CA 92674-9207 (video available in Cantonese and Mandarin)
1-800-432-1997

Ambassadors for Christ (AFC)
MC Lit. Dept. P.O. Box 969
Paradise, PA 17564
888-462-5481
email: mclit@afcinc.org, website: www.idsonline.com/afc/

Bridges International
PO Box 1979    1-206-744-0321
Lynnwood, WA  98046-1979
Bilingual Campus Crusade literature and basic evangelism and
discipleship messages on cassette in Mandarin.

Overseas Campus Magazine
PO Box 638    1-310-325-7968
Lomita, CA 90717    Internet:  http://www.ccim.org/Publishing/OC/
Excellent magazine in Chinese for PRC students.

OMF International
10 West Dry Creek Circle    1-800-422-5330
Littleton, CO  80120-4413    Apologetic booklets.

Moody Institute of Science    1-800-842-1223
E-mail: 73041.3116@compuserve.com    Videos, many available in Mandarin
and Cantonese, about evidence for God in creation.

InterVarsity Press
1-800-843-9487 www.ivpress.com
*Passport to the Bible: An Explorer's Guide.* 24 investigative studies for internationals
on God, humankind, Jesus Christ and experiencing God, written by a team of
international student workers, available from IVP in 1999

## Websites:

www.bridgesinternational.com/menus/apologetics.html
Testimonies and apologetics articles of particular interest to PRC citizens, Bridges
International is a ministry of Campus Crusade.
www. reasons.org
Answers all kinds of apologetics questions but specializes in science-related
questions.  Reasons to Believe was founded by respected astronomer Hugh Ross.
www.gateman.com/acmi
Website of the Association of Christians Ministering to Internationals, resources,
links to Bibles on the Net and to Christian material in many languages.

# Appendix B: Broken Family Diagrams

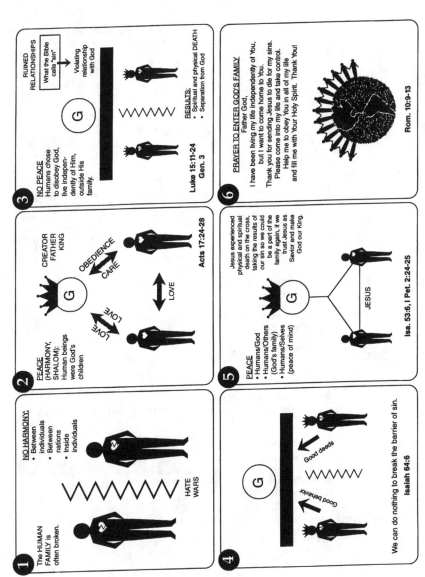

**1.** The HUMAN FAMILY is often broken.

NO HARMONY:
- Between individuals
- Between nations
- Inside individuals

HATE
WARS

**2.** CREATOR FATHER KING

OBEDIENCE
CARE
LOVE
LOVE
LOVE

PEACE (HARMONY, SHALOM): Human beings were God's children

Acts 17:24-28

**3.** RUINED RELATIONSHIPS

What the Bible calls "sin"

→ Violating relationship with God

NO PEACE
Humans chose to disobey God, live independently of Him, outside His family.

Luke 15:11-24
Gen. 3

RESULTS:
- Spiritual and physical DEATH
- Separation from God

**4.** Good behavior
Good deeds

We can do nothing to break the barrier of sin.

Isaiah 64:6

**5.** Jesus experienced physical and spiritual death on the cross, taking the results of our sin so we could be a part of the family again, if we trust Jesus as Savior and make God our King.

JESUS

PEACE
- Humans/God
- Humans/Others (God's family)
- Humans/Selves (peace of mind)

Isa. 53:6, I Pet. 2:24-25

**6.** PRAYER TO ENTER GOD'S FAMILY
Father God,
I have been living my life independently of You, but I want to come home to You.
Thank you for sending Jesus to die for my sins. Please come into my life and take control.
Help me to obey You in all of my life and fill me with Your Holy Spirit. Thank You!

Rom. 10:9-13

# Appendix C: Suggestions For Using Broken Family Diagrams

*NOTE: These diagrams are not intended as a "one-shot" gospel presentation but as a way of giving newcomers to the Bible the big picture. The sinner's prayer is included, however, because people who have already heard parts of the gospel are occasionally ready to accept the Lord once the entire message is explained to them in a chronological fashion. The handout may be placed in a Bible after you have explained it and may be given along with a free Bible. Hopefully, it will be read over and over, with the sinner's prayer available when the person is ready to follow Jesus. The separate frames may also be used to introduce weekly Bible studies (using transparencies) until all are presented. Then the handout can be given out as a review. Or, if you think drawing the figures yourself would make the presentation more personal, you may do that.*

1. The first frame starts with the state of the world and humankind today and does not include a Bible reference. You may talk about the brokenness inside the hearts of individuals, between persons and between nations. Usually people will agree that this is an accurate picture of things.

2. The second frame gives the Bible's picture of the way God intended things and the way they were in the beginning. Note that the crown is on God's head and that there is no brokenness inside human hearts or between individuals and between God and humans. God cared for people, and they responded by obedience. You may talk about the meaning of the Hebrew word *shalom* (peace, wholeness, well-being in the presence of God and His people). Acts 17:24-28 or Genesis 1 are good passages to use with this frame.

3. Frame 3 presents sin and its results. Note that the crown is no longer on God's head, but is on the heads of both humans instead, with alienation resulting between humans and God, inside the hearts of humans and between individuals. The thick black bar represents sin, which can be explained as violating relationship with God. The attitude of the younger son in Luke 15:11-24, independence of the father and the family, may also be used to define sin here, or Genesis 3 may be used. Spiritual death may be defined as separation from God.

4. Frame 4 points out that humans often try to break the barrier between us and God by good works, good behavior, or other methods. But since God is 100% pure and we can never be 100% pure, we can never pierce the barrier. If someone is to break the barrier, it must be God.

5. And that is what He did by sending his son Jesus to die on the cross, taking on both physical and spiritual death, the results of our sin. The outcome is a restoration of peace with God, others and self for those who trust Jesus as Savior and make God their King. Note that the crown is back on God's head and the hearts are no longer broken.

6. Frame 6 is the sinner's prayer with God's family depicted as a worldwide family. Romans 10:9-13 may be used to talk about inviting Jesus into one's life. Revelation 7:9-10 may be used to present the picture of the worldwide family of God. You may say that you do not necessarily expect a person to pray that prayer today, since all that has been presented is so new. But you wanted to provide the big picture and when they are ready to follow Jesus, this is a prayer they can use.

7. Of course this presentation should be tailored to meet the needs of each individual, some will resonate with personal brokenness more, while others will respond to the alienation between nations. Stop to answer questions as you present each frame. For some, it might be better to present one frame per week along with a Bible study.

## Notes

[1] Jim Mann, "China's Lost Generation," *Los Angeles Times Magazine*, March 25, 1990: 10-38.

[2] Stacey Bieler, "Intellectuals in the People's Republic of China, 1980-1988," (1988), 1. Unpublished paper presented to Carol Lee Hamrin, Institute of Chinese Studies, Pasadena, CA. Files of author.

[3] Lectures for MT551, "Conversion," Fuller Theological Seminary (Spring quarter, 1990).

[4] Longji Sun, "The Deep Structure of Chinese Culture," in *Seeds of Fire: Chinese Voices of Conscience*, eds. Geremie Barmè and John Minford (Hong Kong: Far Eastern Economic Review Ltd., 1986) 32.

[5] Norie L. Roeder, "Ministering to Students from Mainland China," (1989), 23. Unpublished paper presented to Sherwood Lingenfelter, Biola University.

[6] Francis L. K. Hsu and Gordon C. Chu, "Changes in Chinese Culture: What Do We Really Know?" in Gordon C. Chu and Francis L. K. Hsu, eds., *Moving a Mountain: Cultural Change in China* (Honolulu: East-West Center, 1979), 414.

[7] Francis L. K. Hsu, *The Study of Literate Civilizations* (New York: Holt & Rinehart and Winston, 1969).

[8] Chu and Hsu, *Moving a Mountain: Cultural Changes in China.*

[9] Ibid., 412-415.

[10] Charles H. Kraft, "Worldview, Paradigms, Power and Bible Translation," (1986), 64. In course reader for "Conversion," Pasadena, CA: Fuller Theological Seminary.

[11] Katie J. Rawson, "Worldview and Worldview Change among International Students: A Model," (1986). Unpublished paper presented to Paul Hiebert, Fuller Theological Seminary, Pasadena, CA.

[12] Xiao-Chun Chen, "The Smell of a Changing China: Reflections on Returning to Beijing," *World Christian*, February, 1990: 21.

[13] Ibid., 23.

[14] Anthony F. C. Wallace, "Revitalization Movements," *American Anthropologist*, 58 (1956): 264-281.

[15] Charles H. Kraft, *Christianity in Culture* (Maryknoll, NY: Orbis Books, 1979), 148-155.

[16] Jacob A. Loewen, "The Indigenous Church and Resocialization," in *Culture and Human Values: Christian Intervention in Anthropological Perspective* (Pasadena, CA: William Carey, 1975).

[17] Charles H. Kraft, *Christianity with Power: Your Worldview and Your Experience of the Supernatural* (Ann Arbor, MI: Servant, 1989), 72.

[18] Glenn Tinder, "Can We Be Good Without God? The Political Meaning of Christianity," *Atlantic Monthly*, December 1989: 69-85.

[19] Zongren Liu, Two Years in the Melting Pot: *The Adventures of a Chinese Newsman in America* (San Francisco: China Books, 1984), 136-147.

[20] Parris H. Chang, "Children's Literature and Political Socialization," in Gordon C. Chu and Francis L. K. Hsu, eds., *Moving a Mountain: Cultural Change in China* (Honolulu: East-West Center, 1979), 238.

[21] J. I. Packer, "The Gospel: Its Content and Communication, A Theological Perspective," in J. R. W. Stott and Robert Coote, eds., *Down to Earth: Studies in Christianity and Culture* (Grand Rapids, MI: Eerdmans Publishing Company, 1980), 103-109.

[22] Ibid., 106.

[23] Anne Thurston, "The Dragon Stirs," *The Wilson Quarterly* Spring: 31-32.

[24] Jimmy Long, *Generating Hope: A Strategy For Reaching the Postmodern Generation* (Downers Grove, IL: InterVarsity Press, 1997a), 69.

[25] J. Richard Middleton and Brian J. Walsh, *Truth Is Stranger Than It Used to Be: Biblical Faith in a Postmodern Age* (Downers Grove, IL: InterVarsity Press, 1955), 29-55.

[26] Thurston, 15.

[27] Lesslie Newbigin, *The Gospel in a Pluralist Society* (Grand Rapids, MI: Eerdmans, 1989), 228-229.

[28] Katie J. Rawson, "Evangelizing East Asian Students in the United States with Special Reference to Media Tools." D.Miss. dissertation, Fuller Theological Seminary, 1999.

[29] Norman C. Kraus, *Jesus Christ our Lord: Christology from a Disciple's Perspective* (Scottdale, PA: Herald Press, 1987), 166-225.

[30] Rawson (1999).

[31] Dallas Willard, *The Divine Conspiracy: Rediscovering Our Hidden Life in God* (San Francisco: Harper San Francisco), 214, 341.

# Critical Points in the Conversion Process

*Samuel Ling*

Recent experience in ministry among mainland Chinese intellectuals (PRCs) has alerted many colleagues to the urgency of evangelism. Some experienced PRC ministry workers are noting unique characteristics about the conversion and discipleship process among PRCs. This leads us to rethink the nature of the evangelistic process itself in light of Scripture.

## Holistic Faith and Repentance

Both the Chinese church and the American church have grown accustomed to an experiential or emotion-based transformation experience, which we call "conversion." We speak of a *decision* to *accept* Jesus Christ. Often the decision is expressed by an act, the act to "pray to receive Christ." Sometimes the conversion is very dramatic.

Most Christians agree that just an intellectual presentation of the gospel truths, and giving consent to them, does not make a person a Christian. Thus the emotional and volitional aspects of faith are emphasized, while the intellectual aspect is relegated to the background as only a prelude to faith. One result of this neglect of the role of *understanding* in saving faith is that many contemporary evangelical Christians have very weak doctrinal convictions, and many are biblically illiterate.

In confronting the minds of many PRCs, however, we are forced to engage in apologetics. Many non-PRC Christians involved in evangelism find that PRCs are far superior in their ability at argumentation. We must be prepared to answer to dialectical materialism, atheism and evolution. We need to read books with them, discuss questions, and wait upon them as they, by the grace of God, reconstruct a new worldview. We are discovering that it often takes a long time for a PRC to think and rethink the claims of Christ. Thus we are rediscovering the importance of the *intellectual* aspect of faith, i.e., the role of understanding.

What is faith? In traditional Christian theology, faith involves cognition (*notitia*), conviction (*assensus*), and commitment (*fiducia*). In the words of the Westminster Assembly (1643-1647):

> Justifying faith is a saving grace, wrought in the heart of a sinner by the spirit and word of God, whereby he, being *convinced* of his sin and misery, and of the disability in himself and all other creatures to recover him out of his lost condition, not only *assenteth* to the truth of the promise of the gospel, but *receiveth* and *resteth* upon Christ and his righteousness, therein held forth, for pardon of sin, and for the accepting and accounting of his person righteous in the sight of God for salvation (Larger Catechism, Question 72; italics mine).

Note that the (intellectual) assenting to the truth of the promise of the gospel, and (heart-felt) conviction about his need, are every bit as essential to faith as the (decision involving) receiving and resting upon Jesus Christ. There is no dichotomy; there is no truncating of faith.

Similarly, repentance has an intellectual, emotional, and volitional aspect as well. In the words of the Shorter Catechism:

> Repentance unto life is a saving grace, whereby a sinner, out of a true *sense* of his sin, and *apprehension* of the mercy of God in Christ, doth, with *grief* and *hatred* of his sin, *turn* from it unto God, with full purpose of, and endeavour after, new obedience. (Question 87; italics mine)

Note again, there is a true sense and understanding (apprehension) of man's sin and God's grace and mercy in Christ. One feels grief and hatred for one's own sin and finally makes the decision to turn from sin to God. The commitment is to a new lifestyle of obedience.

## Critical Questions

Not only are we discovering that PRCs take time to think out their faith, but some of them may have actually "made a commitment to Christ" (to use our non-PRC, Western evangelical language) without openly acknowledging their faith before others. Baptism is a particularly sensitive subject for those who desire to return to China. In light of these and other complications in the conversion process, when may we say that a person has become a Christian?

Traditionally, fundamentalists and evangelicals use the act of believing (profession of faith and repentance) as the measuring point of "being born again." Is this adequate? If conversion is a process, this is true not only of PRCs, but of children of Christian parents (who take years of nurture prior to a personal commitment acknowledged before others), and of many who through searching the Scriptures finally come to the point of commitment. When is a person born again?

## Regeneration

It is helpful to break down the question into four questions. First, when does the Holy Spirit regenerate a person (Ezekiel 36:25, 26, 27; John 3:3; Titus 3:5)? When does God take away that heart of stone and replace it with the heart of flesh in a person? When does a person become new and born again (II Corinthians 5:17)? For many people, these are mysteries. The Holy Spirit moves as the wind blows; we can only see the effects.

Logically (not always chronologically), however, the work of regeneration, the new birth wrought by the Holy Spirit, occurs before faith and repentance. Humanity is at enmity with God. Only by grace alone through faith alone (and faith is a gift from God, Ephesians 2:8-9), are we turned around in order that we are capable and willing to repent of our sins and trust in Christ. God "made us alive" (Ephesians 2:5). In the case of many children born into Christian homes, who later in life make a personal commitment to Christ, this work of regeneration is a mystery and a process. Some people give testimonies (and they are legitimate testimonies — some evangelicals tend to judge such testimonies as "nominal Christian," but they need not be) like the following: "I never knew that I was not a Christian. Ever since I knew anything as a young child, I knew that Jesus died for my sins, He is my savior, and my sins are forgiven." Through years of nurture by family and church, by the work of the Holy Spirit, the person comes to an assurance of salvation. And so it is with many PRCs!

Actually we should adjust our terminology so that we do not speak of a person as being "born again" on such and such a date. This only confuses the issue. What often happens on "such and such a date," is that a person acknowledges his or her faith in Christ; or that he or she is baptized.

## Faith and Repentance

This brings us to the second question: When does a person turn in faith and repentance to Jesus Christ? Traditionally evangelicals think of this as a point in time, a crisis-event in response to the preaching of the gospel or the reading of Scripture. This indeed is the experience of many Christians and we praise God for crusade evangelism, evangelistic preaching in the local church, and Christian literature distribution. Having said that, however, it remains true that faith and repentance are both "saving graces." In other words, they are God-given gifts. If faith is a God-given gift, then God may give it in such a way that we may detect it at the moment it is given, or we may not discover it until a later point in time.

For many PRCs, faith and repentance occurs very quietly in the privacy of their minds and hearts. Only God knows the human heart. Our duty as Christians is to preach the gospel faithfully, clearly, completely, gently and reverently (I Peter 3:15), and pray that the seed of the word of God will grow (Matthew 13). And God intends to make his word effective (Isaiah 55:8-11)!

One day, a young lady went to her pastor in Scotland and said, "Pastor, there is this fellow student in our Conservatory of Music. He says he wants to become a Christian." The pastor made an appointment to see the young man. The student came and said, "I don't know what is happening in my life. I used to have no interest in prayer; I have a great desire to pray now. I used to have no interest in the Bible; I have an urge the study the Bible now." And on it went. The pastor's response: "They said you wanted to become a Christian. Why, you already are one!" (Story related by Eric Alexander, address on "Regeneration," Philadelphia Conference on Reformed Theology.)

Regeneration is mysterious, and may be a process. Faith, too, is a mystery, and may involve a process. But the fruit tells the tale!

## Assurance

The fact that regeneration, as well as faith, are processes in many cases does not excuse Christians from remaining faithful in "friendship evangelism" with an excessive hesitation at "proclamation evangelism." After all, faith comes from hearing! However, what is the goal of evangelism? I would like to submit that the gospel is not so much the *profession of faith* (praying to receive Christ). The end is assurance (I John 5:13): that the person may know that he or she has eternal life (cf. D. James Kennedy's *Evangelism Explosion*).

Thus, the third question is: When does a person gain assurance of his or her salvation? When does a person know that he or she has eternal life, is justified and accepted by God? This, too, involves a process.

In the visible church there are people who should not have assurance, but think that they do. These people presume on God's goodness while in fact they have not been born again. Then there are people who have made a genuine profession of faith in Christ—or more accurately, who have been regenerated by the Holy Spirit—and yet do not have assurance of their salvation. This may be due to: (a) ignorance of the promises of God; (b) a tender conscience; (c) sin in a person's life; or (d) negligence to make use of the means God has ordained for spiritual growth (e.g. the Word, preaching of the Word, prayer, worship, fellowship and the Lord's Supper).

Nevertheless, "such as truly believe in the Lord Jesus, and love Him in sincerity, endeavouring to walk in all good conscience before Him, may, in this life, be certainly assured that they are in the state of grace, and may rejoice in the hope of the glory of God, which hope shall never make them ashamed" (Westminster Confession of Faith, 18:1). This assurance may be shaken or weakened, yet those who truly belong to Jesus shall never be snatched out of Jesus'—and the Father's—hand (John 10:28, 29). Assurance of faith is a blessing, but it is not essential to saving faith. A true believer may struggle to gain assurance for a long time. For PRCs as well as for many others, assurance, too, is a process. There is much hope in this process, however, for everyone with sincere faith in, and love for, the Lord Jesus.

## Incorporation into the Church

Is everything, then, a process? This brings us to the fourth question: When is a person incorporated into the visible Body of Christ, the church? For Christians over the centuries, the point in time is baptism for adult believers. Churches which practice infant baptism provide an opportunity for a grown child to profess his or her faith in Christ before the congregation. At this point evangelical Christians have a lot to learn from the typical non-Christian Chinese person. Somehow, the non-Christian knows instinctively the importance of baptism. Thus the conversation goes like this:

| Christian: | Are you a Christian? |
|---|---|
| *"Non-Christian":* | *No, I am not.* |
| Christian: | Have you accepted Christ as your Savior? |
| *"Non-Christian":* | *Oh yes, but I have not been baptized yet.* |

Somehow the non-Christian, and the new (but not yet baptized) Christian understands the importance of baptism more clearly than the average evangelical Christian does! We have taken baptism so lightly; we call it only a ceremony, merely a ritual. The early church, and the church throughout the centuries, has taken baptism much more seriously.

Many PRCs hesitate to be baptized. May we take this as an extraordinary circumstance? If so, what are the requirements for taking the Lord's Supper? What does it mean to be able to "discern the body of the Lord" (I Corinthians 11:29)?

The early church provided for a period of time during which a new convert — an inquirer — prepares for baptism. During this phase he or she was instructed in the doctrines of Scripture. Should we reconsider such a category for new believers? This process may last for months, or even a year or two.

If we take the church — the visible, local congregation — as seriously as God takes it, we will also have to take baptism more seriously. And we will then turn to help those who prepare for baptism, even if this preparation process might take several years.

Ministry among PRCs challenges the evangelical Christian to prepare adequately. We need to study apologetics, church history, and the doctrines of the Christian faith, including our understanding of regeneration, faith, assurance and baptism. This may take us to a renewed understanding of, and commitment to, the glorious ministry of the Word of God in the visible church.

# "Evening Chats" in North America

*Stacey Bieler*

## Introduction

Some of our PRC friends residing in North America are too skeptical to attend Bible studies but are eager to discuss the implications of Christianity on society. "Evening chats" with our friends can go a long way to dispel myths about Christianity and to build understanding of the tremendous impact Christianity can have on Chinese society. PRCs can be engaged in conversation in a variety of topics. We will first address two *practical* topics about living in the United States: (1) marriage and family and (2) work. Next, two *philosophical* topics about the future of China will be introduced: (1) politics, and (2) economics. Many of our friends are more interested in the practical topics because they are focused on attaining a piece of the American Dream, but the question about how to reform China still haunts most of them.

These topics offer Christians an opportunity to share about the kingdom of God. Long-term friendships keep us from feeling pressured to cover all the gospel in one sitting, since we know we will have another opportunity to have another opportunity to converse. We can use these issues as a way to attract students into a deeper study of the Christian faith.

The idea for "conversations" comes from two sources. When Matteo Ricci (1552-1610) was a Jesuit missionary in China, he realized that China's intellectuals were unprepared for Christianity. He understood that he first needed "to win for Christianity an accepted place in Chinese life." "I do not think that we shall establish a church, but instead a room for discussion and we will say Mass privately in another chapel, because one preaches more effectively and with greater fruit here through conversation than through formal sermons."[1] Perry Link, an American professor from Princeton University, lived in China from 1988 to 1989. His book, *Evening Chats in Beijing*, offers us an opportunity to listen in on Chinese intellectuals' discussions about their role in society, Chinese education, the future of China, and the like. We can tell our friends that Christianity has many important things to say about Chinese culture and about the future of China as a nation.

These themes are not only useful when talking with your friends from China individually, but also when choosing a Bible study series, topics for a large group meeting, a movie, or a piece of drama to perform.[2] Since we cannot be experts on all of these topics, we will need to find people within the Christian community who can address these issues.[3] This will offer an opportunity for our Chinese friends to meet a variety of Christians and see how Christians can disagree, but still love and respect one another.

All of these topics need to be approached with great humility. None of us have perfect marriages, families, or political or economic systems. The gospel of God's grace and transforming power has much to say to *all* of us, individually and corporately.

## Marriage and Family

Several factors may influence the high divorce rate among our Chinese friends in the United States. They feel stress from living in another culture where their families are not available to encourage and offer support. Some take advantage of the freedom to escape from unhappy marriages. Some are separated by choice from their spouse (e.g. studying in two different places), while other marriages are strained when one member adjusts better to North America than the other (often due to English proficiency). Those who were children during the Cultural Revolution (1966-1976) often lack good family models of trust and reconciliation.

One possible panel discussion could look at the sources of common marital struggles in America. Christians should speak honestly about their experiences. They should tell how God has answered their prayers and brought healing to their marriages. Walter Wangerin's book, *As for Me and My House* has been very encouraging for several of our friends. The book focuses on the heart of marriage, the practice of forgiving one another. Though our friends were not Christians they had the same ideal view of marriage that the book strongly supports. One friend said, "I wish I had known about the book earlier." Another wrote, "That book you gave me is priceless. Even though our marriage didn't work out, I still believe what is said in it is true." She became a Christian a year later.

Raising children in North America is often confusing since our Chinese friends do not always have their parents around for guidance. As friends, we do not need to be married or have children to be drawn into these discussions! We can share about our own experience of being raised in the United States and we can help them know how to respond to pressures within American culture. Once time we met a friend at the grocery store and she told us how her third grade son had brought home some pornographic literature which his American friend had given him. Shocked and worried since she had never seen such material in China, she asked us for suggestions. We commiserated with her and encouraged her to talk with her son.

Invite a panel of parents to come and share their stories about raising a family. The panel could consist of parents who are presently raising their children, and parents who already have grown children. Both can offer examples and encouragement. Raising children can be difficult, especially in an American culture where the parents' authority often clashes with the child's desire for freedom and individualism. Kevin Huggins' *Parenting Adolescents* is a difficult book to read because it advocates that parents need to change more than their children! This book has helped friends who are desperate to be good parents and understand their children.

Our friends also learn about marriage and family by observing us in our homes. They see how we love and listen to our children. They watch how we discipline and forgive them. How do you teach your children to love and share with others? All parents face these struggles.

We can talk about the values which our Father wishes to instill in His children. The fruit of the Spirit are qualities we admire in people and wish we had. Besides looking at passages which discuss each individual fruit (e.g. love, peace, joy), our Bible studies examine passages which describe the process and the inherent tensions of bearing such fruit (See Appendix A).

Marriage and family crises often open up opportunities for deep conversations. You may be shy about speaking about your faith, but take these opportunities to say, "As a Christian, I believe ..." We all fail at loving, but we can talk about God as the model of a good Father who loves, corrects and forgives us.

## Work

Looking for work is stressful enough for people who have grown up in North America! It can be especially difficult for our

Chinese friends who grew up assuming that they would be assigned jobs by the government. In the United States some have the unrealistic expectation that their advisors will find jobs for them.

Job-searching skills can be taught on an individual basis or in groups. They could include: writing resumes, editing cover letters, learning what questions to expect at an interview, learning what questions to ask (a new idea for many), and balancing various offers.

If they are applying for an academic position, it may be helpful to offer your friends an opportunity to practice their presentation. Since most likely these positions entail teaching judgmental undergraduates, spend time helping your friend improve their language skills. One Chinese friend appreciated the time we gave to help her develop her interviewing skills and to describe how search processes are conducted. She was particularly grateful for our prayers since those were stressful times for her because she did not have any family in the United States to lean on.

Keeping a job is just as important. Invite a panel of business people to talk about such issues as: becoming a valued employee; work expectations; setting boundaries for work, family, and other obligations; how to deal with an abusive workplace; and working as a team.

One semester we asked people from church to speak to our international Sunday school class. They talked about how they became Christians and what difference it makes at work because they are Christians. This series yielded several benefits. People in the church were given an opportunity to reflect about how God had worked in their lives. They also were able to interact with internationals. Internationals heard Americans share how God had an active role in people's lives. Many speakers, unbeknownst to one another, shared a common life verse: "Trust in the Lord with all your heart, and do not lean on your own understanding. In all your ways acknowledge Him and He will make your paths straight" (Proverbs 3:4-5). This made a great impression on competent internationals who thought that they had to succeed by their own will and power.

Students can come to see how Christians serve their King by living out the Good News of the Kingdom — servant leadership, joy, and trust — in the work place.

## Politics

Our Chinese friends are interested in Christianity not only for individual reasons, such as personal salvation or guidance with family and work, but for its possible role in changing society. Some may be looking for a source of values since they recognize that any society needs a basis for morality. Do not be surprised if their interest in Christianity may be for purely pragmatic reasons: How can God be used to create a new society? We can pray that they may find out *how God wants to use them* to build a greater society, His kingdom!

Some of our friends may be enamored with the word "democracy" and see it only in terms of freedom, rather than seeing the foundations, weaknesses, and responsibilities inherent in a democracy. We who belong to the Kingdom of God should be the first to point out weaknesses within a democracy. For example, the idea of liberty is abused when people focus on their rights rather than on their responsibilities. Like Abraham, we are "looking forward to the city with foundations, whose architect and builder is God" (Hebrews 12:10). We can help them to see that their dreams cannot be fulfilled in any political system. Chinese students may be sensitive to critiques of Chinese political culture if American culture is not similarly critiqued. Some of the questions about politics and societal change include:

## What are the necessary foundations for democracy?

One foundation is the belief in the worth of each individual. This is wonderfully described in Glenn Tinder's book, *The Political Meaning of Christianity*. He shows how the idea of the created and redeemed individual is foundational to the hope, liberty and social transformation that our Chinese friends are searching for.

Another foundation for democracy is having or creating a "public sphere," a place to speak outside of government control. Both the playwright Vaclav Havel in Czechoslovakia and Lech Walesa, who combined the unions and the Catholic church in Poland, offered an alternative voice to their government's propaganda. The history and possibility of creating a public sphere in China was hotly debated in the early 1990s since it was seen as key to reform in China. (See *Modern China*, July 1990, 309-329 and the entire April 1993 issue.) The Chinese Communist Party continues to arrest Christians in China because it sees Christianity as presenting an alternative worldview.

A third foundation of democracy is law. The supremacy of the law means that no one is exempt due to wealth, political standing or connections. One semester our international Bible Study examined the life of David. When Nathan the prophet confronted King David about taking another man's wife and killing her husband, David recognized that he had broken God's laws and asked God for forgiveness (2 Samuel 11-12). Being king did not exempt David from God's laws. The cathedral in Aachen, Germany was the site of twenty-nine coronations of German kings from 936 to 1531. As each king began his earthly rule, he looked across the cathedral to a cross, which was to remind him that he was still under the watch of the Heavenly King. Though kings and clergy did not always acted Christianly, the alternative, having no God and no rules, has been a source of great suffering during this century. Paul Johnson introduces his book, *Modern Times*, with these words:

> [T]he decline and ultimately the collapse of the religious impulse would leave a huge vacuum. The history of modern times is in great part the history of how that vacuum had been filled. . . . Those who had once filled the ranks of the totalitarian clergy would become totalitarian politicians. And above all, the Will to Power would produce a new kind of messiah, *uninhibited by any religious sanctions whatever*, and with an unappeasable appetite for controlling mankind.[4]

Education is another foundation for democracy. A voting citizenship needs to be able to read and write in order to make choices. What is the role of education? Is it supposed to create a knowledgeable citizenry, build a technical workforce, or teach ethics to the next generation? Can education bring about ethical behavior in and of itself? (People in the West are educated, but are they moral?) Though our friends may be enamored with democracy, the reality is that China is still 70% peasants. How can they be prepared to participate in a democratic system?

Related questions are "How did democracy arise in the West?" Were the conditions unique? Why has democracy been so difficult to transfer to other countries during this century? How can a ruler remain righteous when "absolute power corrupts absolutely?" How can our friends sustain their hope as change agents in the face of difficulties and not become corrupt themselves as they gain power?

## What role has Christianity played in American democracy?

Some Christians overstate the influence of Christianity on the founding fathers of the U.S. as an overreaction to those historians who deny that Christianity has had no influence in American history. Neither extreme is helpful. The Europeans came to America looking for both religious freedom and monetary gain. One book that describes this inherent tension in American history is Robert Bellah's *The Broken Covenant*. In *This Rebellious House* Steven Keillor argues that our nation has never been a "Christian" one, but then goes on to show the influence of Christianity on our history. Ask a church historian (professional or not!) to speak about the influence of Christianity in society, such as the Great Awakenings (1740-60; 1790s), or the social reform movements, such as the abolition of slavery, during the decades before the Civil War.

## How has Christianity brought transformation around the world?

The Bible offers us an example of the church in the first century. When we studied the book of Acts, we asked: what difference does Christianity make? We looked at Christianity's impact on society: new power, leaders, rules, and economic relations, not just new hearts. (See Appendix B.)

A historical series could present biographies of reformers:

- Francis of Assisi's confronting the power and wealth of the thirteenth century Catholic church
- William Wilberforce's role in stopping England's participation in the slave trade
- William Carey's influence in India in stopping the burning of widows
- John Wesley's call to revival and social reform in eighteenth century England.

Common questions could be addressed in each case. What motivated the reformers? At what speed and at what cost did the reform movement proceed? Where did they begin their reforms: from the top down or from the bottom up? What methods did they use?

## What are the weaknesses of democracies in the West?

First, the United States is suffering from individualism, alienation and division. Individualism is sometimes quite appealing to our friends who have felt stifled by a society which emphasizes community. Robert Bellah, a professor at the University of California at Berkeley, and four other scholars wrote in *Habits of the Heart* about the drawbacks of individualism. They told how Alexis de Tocqueville, a Frenchman who traveled in the United States in the 1830s, warned in *Democracy in America* about the results of rampant individualism. He defined the mores or "habits of the heart" as notions, opinions and ideas that shape mental habits.

> He stresses throughout the book that their mores have been the key to the Americans' success in establishing and maintaining a free republic and that undermining American mores is the most certain road to undermining the free institutions of the United States....The habits and practices of religion and democratic participation educate the citizen to a larger view than his purely private world would allow. [5]

Tocqueville warned that if the social mores were weakened, the people would become isolated from one another. Associational life, such as church life, was the best protection against "the mass society of mutually antagonistic individuals [which become] easy prey to despotism."[6]

Another weakness in American life is that many Americans do not participate in civic duties, such as voting. They believe that politics is either too corrupt or too distant to be worth investment of their time or energy. Americans are withdrawing from the public square just as people elsewhere, such as former East Germans and black South Africans, are eagerly exercising the rights to vote.

## How does a Christian participate in culture?

Christians have answered this question across a wide continuum of responses over the centuries. Richard Niebuhr's *Christ and Culture* describes five responses of the church through the ages: Christ against culture, the Christ of culture, Christ above culture, Christ and culture in paradox, and Christ the transformer of culture. Some Christians are so much in the world that they lose their distinctiveness, while others withdraw from the world because they regard it as inherently evil. Many Christians experience great tension of being salt and light (Matthew 5:13-16), of being in the world, but not of it (John 15:19). James Boice's book, *Two Cities, Two Loves: Christian Responsibility in a Crumbling Culture* argues for the need for Christians to transform their culture.

Welcome your friends' questions about politics and societal change as opportunities to speak about the only wise and loving King who wants his family, the church community, to extend his Kingdom in all dimensions of their lives.

## Economics

The Chinese Communists promised a just economic system, but it was not efficient. Our friends in the United States see the gap between rich and poor and question the benefits of capitalism

207

while eagerly partaking in them. Under Deng Xiaopeng's policy, "to get rich is glorious," the gap between rich and poor in China continues to widen as people take advantage of their connections. The difference between poorer inland and richer coastal areas in China makes this broken promise of justice intolerable and threatens to destabilize the country.

## What does economics assume about human nature?

The field of economics assumes that people are selfish and individualistic. They will pursue their own interests and are not altruistic. Economics gives us insight into sinfulness and corroborates with God's view that we need a heart-change in order to care for others. The Bible helps us to speak realistically with those who hope to create a new society and new people now.

## What is the best trade-off between economic efficiency and economic equality?

When there are stronger incentives to work harder, save more and/or invest more, there will be an increase in productivity, national output and personal income. In order to provide stronger incentives for success in the economic game, however, the gaps between the "winners" and the "losers" must necessarily be widened. For it is this gap that provides the incentives. In every society, there is a trade-off between economic efficiency and economic equality. Stronger incentives for economic success leads to a more efficient economy, but also a greater inequality of incomes.

In the United States, the gap between the rich and the poor is larger than in many other advanced countries. For example, Sweden has far less income inequality. The income inequality in the United States has been increasing over time, as most of the benefits of economic growth in the last twenty years have gone to the top 10% of the population. Has America gone too far in the direction of emphasizing economic efficiency at the expense of equality? How much does economic inequality contribute to poorer education and increased crime in the United States?

## What does the Bible say about justice?

Is justice important to God? To us? As Christians we need to admit to having blinders to many Bible passages about money because we do not want to obey them. Often we also have blinders to people who are in need.

The Old Testament law and prophets called God's people to care for the weak and poor in their society: the widows, the orphans and the aliens (Deuteronomy 10: 18; Amos 5:11-12). When God told the Israelites to celebrate his goodness every fifty years (Jubilee) by dismantling all inequalities, he promised that they would live securely in the land (Leviticus 25). Their disobedience against the Lord resulted in captivity and exile for seventy years, so that the land could enjoy an overdue rest (Jeremiah 29:10; 2 Chronicles 36:21).

Jesus warns that only those who care for the hungry, thirsty, stranger, sick, or prisoner will enter the Kingdom of Heaven (Matthew 25: 31-46). God's call to be merciful is a stunning alternative to the powerful protecting their power. Compassion is based on God's view that people are created in His image; they are not *things* to be used.

## How is the Church responding to injustice in society?

How has the church restrained capitalism's excesses? Some

denominations are much more active in offering social services, such as the Catholics or Lutherans. Invite people who can explain their motivation for participating in ministries such as homeless shelters, Habitat for Humanity, and sponsoring children overseas. Others have heard a call to work at the national rather than local level, such as members of Evangelicals for Social Action.

An upper-class student from Latin America went to a talk for internationals by a man whose organization provides both physical and spiritual help for the poor. When he spoke about the poor in her country, her eyes were opened to the fact that they were people rather than just "scenery." After becoming a Christian and graduating, she became the director for the organization in her country.

How do God's values impact the ways in which Christians make choices about spending their money? This topic may seem too personal to us, but it can help our international friends understand priorities in Christians' lives.

Go beyond our friends' search for an efficient and just economic system. Tell them about a just and merciful King who cares for each person He has created and who calls His followers to just relationships with their neighbors.

## Conclusion

Conversations with Chinese friends are treasures to be cherished. By listening and learning to appreciate their personal and philosophical struggles, we open ourselves to opportunities to show them how God, not earthly institutions, can fill their deepest desires. Each of us needs God's transforming power to give us new and soft hearts so we can be loving in our families, responsible in our work, righteous in our places of influence, and just in our relationships.

# Appendix A:
## *The Fruit of the Spirit*

| | | |
|---|---|---|
| 1. | The Fruit of the Spirit | Galatians 5:16-26# |
| 2. | Love | 1 John 4:7-16 |
| 3. | Bearing Fruit that will Last | John 15: 1-17# |
| 4. | Joy | Luke 24:33-53 |
| 5. | Peace | Isaiah 43:1-7 |
| 6. | A Harvest of Righteousness and Peace | Hebrews 12:1-13* |
| 7. | Patience | Matthew 18:21-35 |
| 8. | Kindness | 2 Samuel 9 |
| 9. | Every Good Tree Bears Good Fruit | Matthew 7:15-27* |
| 10. | Goodness | Psalm 107 |
| 11. | Faithfulness | 2 Chronicles 20:1-30 |
| 12. | The Fruit of Light | Ephesians 5:8-20* |
| 13. | Gentleness | 1 Thess 2:1-12 |
| 14. | Self-control | 2 Peter 1:3-10;# 1 Cor 9:19-27 |
| 15. | Bear Fruit to God rather than Death | Romans 7:4-8:4* |
| 16. | Produce Fruit in Keeping with Repentance | Luke 3:1-18* |

*[#We used Fruit of the Spirit, from Inter Varsity Press.*

*\*Additional studies came from Fisherman's Fruit of the Spirit. We added other passages which discussed the method and the tensions of living a Spirit-filled life.]*

## Appendix B:

### *The Book of Acts: Christian Impact on Society*

| | | |
|---|---|---|
| 1. | New Goals in Life | Acts 1: 1-14 |
| 2. | New Power | Acts 2: 1-41 |
| 3. | New Economics | Acts 2:41-47; 4:32-5:11 |
| 4. | New Relationship to Religious Authority | Acts 4:1-31 |
| 5. | New Leadership Qualifications | Acts 5:40 -6:1-7 |
| 6. | New Interpretation of History | Acts 6:8- 7:60 |
| 7. | New Cultures | Acts 8: 26-40 |
| 8. | A New Heart | Acts 7:55-8:3; 9: 1-31 |
| 9. | News: God does not have Favorites | Acts 10 |
| 10. | New Miracles | Acts 12 |
| 11. | New Rules | Acts 15: 1-35; 1 Corinthians 8 |
| 12. | New Teaching: You Can Know God | Acts 17: 16-34 |
| 13. | New Leadership Style | Acts 20: 17-38 |
| 14. | New Boldness Before Political Leaders | Acts 25: 23-26:32 |
| 15. | New Ways to Respond to Crisis | Acts 27- 28:10 |
| 16. | New View of Life and Death | Acts 28; Philippians 1:12-26 |

# Resource List

## Books

Robert Bellah, *The Broken Covenant* (Seabury Press, 1977).

Robert Bellah, et al. *Habits of the Heart* (Harper and Row, 1985).

_____, *The Good Society* (Vintage, 1922).

James Boice, *Two Cities, Two Loves* (Inter Varsity Press, 1996).

Kevin Huggins, *Parenting Adolescents* (Navs Press, 1989)

Paul Johnson, *Modern Times* (Harper and Row, 1983)

Steven Keillor, *This Rebellious House* (Inter Varsity Press, 1996).

Perry Link, *Evening Chats in Beijing* (Norton, 1992).

Richard Niebuhr's *Christ and Culture* (Harper, 1951).

Thomas Oden, *Two Worlds: Notes on the Death of Modernity in America and Russia* (Inter Varsity Press, 1992).

Ben Patterson, *Serving God* (Inter Varsity Press) on worship and work.

John Stott, *The Message of Ephesians* (Inter Varsity Press, 1979).

_____, *The Message of the Sermon on the Mount* (Inter Varsity Press, 1978).

Jorg Swoboda, *The Revolution of the Candles* (Mercer University Press, 800-637-2378, ext. 2880)

Glenn Tinder, *The Political Meaning of Christianity* (Harper Collins, 1991).

Vishal Mangalwadi, *Truth and Social Reform* (contact McLaurin Institute, 1-800-582-8541).

Walter Wangerin, *As for Me and My House* (Thomas Nelson, 1990).

## Bible Studies

*David* (Inter Varsity Press)

*Doing Justice*, Showing Mercy (Fisherman)

*Economic Justice* (Inter Varsity Press)

*Fruit of the Spirit* (Fisherman)

*Loving Justice* (Inter Varsity Press)

*Old Testament Kings* (Inter Varsity Press)

*People and Technology* (Inter Varsity Press)

## OMF Apologetic Booklets *(Order from OMF, 1-800-422-5330)*

*Democracy, Morality and the U.S. Constitution*

*The Socialist Quest for the New Man*

## Movies

| | |
|---|---|
| <u>Family</u> | <u>Politics</u> |
| Tender Mercies | Sacrifice |
| Searching for Bobby Fischer | Citizen Kane |
| <u>Work</u> | <u>Economics</u> |
| Jerry Maguire* | Jean de Florette |
| Chariots of Fire | Howard's End |
| Babette's Feast | |

*Always preview a movie before you show it to a group. This one may have offensive scenes, but it is effective in showing the struggles of a man learning to be responsible in work and relationships.*

## Notes

[1] Simon Leys, *The Burning Forest* (New York: Henry Holt, 1985), 40-41.

[2] Before showing a movie to your international friends, (1) preview the movie, (2) read several reviews, (3) consider your friends' English language ability (4) prepare questions for one or two breaks and at the end of the movie. Stacey Bieler, "Movies as Outreach Tools, " *ACMI Newsletter*, September 1994, 3.

[3] Selection and orientation of panelists calls for careful thought. A written description of the audience should be given to a speaker. Give panel members some written questions so they can prepare answers in advance. The moderator and panel members should meet before the discussion starts to get acquainted and decide who will lead out in answering each question. Katie Rawson, "Using Panels with International Students, " *ACMI Newsletter*, September 1994, 1-2.

[4] Paul Johnson, *Modern Times* (New York: Harper & Row, 1983), 48, emphasis mine.

[5] Robert Bellah et al, *Habits of the Heart: Individualism and Commitment in American Life* (Berkeley: University of California Press, 1996), 37-38.

[6] Ibid., 38.

# Returning To China:
# Push and Pull Factors

*Stacey Bieler*

Today many Chinese students and scholars are staying in the United States after they complete their studies. Since the mid-1980s the issue of non-return has been an irritant in China's dream of gaining expertise through sending students abroad. A variety of factors influence the students' decision to stay in the States or to return to China. Some students are choosing alternatives which keep them in touch with their culture, but allow them to live outside of China.

## Historical Background

The Chinese government began sending students abroad after 1978 as a way to recover from the ten devastating years of the Cultural Revolution (1966-1976), when scholars were sent to the countryside and campuses were closed or politicized. Beginning in 1978, older scholars were sent to the United States for one to two years to gain information quickly in their fields. Since they had received a sound academic foundation in Chinese universities before 1966, the government thought they would be able to help China catch up quickly. Most returned to China due to visa regulations and family connections. After China began allowing graduate students to come to the United States, the Chinese population on U.S.

215

campuses grew quickly, from less than a thousand in 1978-1979 to fourteen thousand in 1984-1985.

In the mid-1980s, students began to show patterns of not returning. Some students had come to the States with the intention of never returning because they had seen their families destroyed during the Cultural Revolution. Others chose to study in Canada because of easier immigration laws. Problems with research facilities in China were also a factor. For example, forty students came in 1982 as part of a program to study chemistry. When the first two received their Ph.D.s in 1985 and returned home, they found there were no teaching jobs and no research laboratories available for them. When the others on the program heard this they decided not to return.[1] Some stayed to continue their academic careers with a hope of eventually returning to China.

Sporadic political campaigns against Western influence in China also caused the students to worry. When the government launched the "Campaign against Spiritual Pollution" in 1983, the students wondered: Would this get out of hand like the Cultural Revolution? Would those who studied abroad be once more considered as traitors to the motherland as an earlier generation of returned students had been accused of during the Cultural Revolution?

In 1987 the government launched another campaign against Bourgeois Liberalism. In February, twelve hundred Chinese students in the United States signed an open letter. Seven hundred used their actual names. They complained about the four reformers, Hu Yaobang, Fang Lizhi, Liu Binyan, and Wang Ruowang, who had been expelled from the party.[2] Liu Binyan wrote:

> The campaign against "bourgeois liberalization" had shattered the last hopes many had had for the country. Soon after my expulsion from the Party had been

announced, an overseas student, with a Ph.D. degree
in mathematics, who had already made preparations
to return to China, had written to me: "I'm not coming
back."[3]

Before 1987 most of the state-sponsored students/scholars returned to China after completing their studies. After 1987, they did not.

The Chinese government became worried that the students were not returning as quickly as it had hoped. This became the most critical issues in discussions between the National Association of Foreign Student Advisors (NAFSA, now called the Association of International Educators) delegations and their Chinese hosts in 1987 and 1988. Misunderstanding over several issues was part of the cause of the problem. The Chinese officials expected the students to only take three years to get a Ph.D. They also believed that foreign student advisors (FSAs) could influence the students' return by appealing to their sense of obligation and responsibility. The NAFSA delegation members did not feel that this was the most effective method nor an appropriate role for FSAs. Instead they encouraged the Chinese government to offer incentives, such as assurances that students would have future opportunities to return to the countries in which they studied for further collaborative research.[4]

## Returning after June 4, 1989

During the spring of 1989, some students in the United States supported the student protesters at Tiananmen Square. They marched in rallies, raised money, and sent faxes into China after the official news blackout. After the crackdown on June 4, many students did not want to return to China because they did not want to condone the government's actions. Others were scared to return home after hearing that the government "ranked" the dissidents' actions and was planning to react accordingly.

When the United States Congress passed the Chinese Student Protection Act in 1992 any Chinese national who had arrived in the States before April 11, 1990 could apply for immigrant status (a green card) and settle permanently in the States. The Act considered everyone as a political refugee rather than only those who had actively protested. One result of the Protection Act was that China lost an important and substantial body of professional personnel. On the other hand, the Chinese government was relieved from the need to deal with returned students demanding changes in the political structure. The Chinese government continued to gain further benefits from students who obtained green cards and had the freedom to help China economically or academically, but did not have to stay in China. In an era of increasing globalization, the concept of "brain drain" has been replaced recently by the term "migration of talent" which reflects the continuing connections that students have with their home countries.

## Reasons Why Students and Scholars Do Not Return to China

Though the exact number for Chinese students in the United States has always been unknown, some say as many as 90% of the students who came to the States have decided to stay here at least for the immediate future. Their decisions are influenced by several factors.

### Politics

A few student activists are afraid of being punished for their outspokenness, but most are enjoying the freedom of politics not impacting every area of life in North America. Most waited to see who would lead China for the long haul. They wondered if Jiang

Zemin would be only a transitional leader or if he could retain his power in the face of strong opponents. The students worried that political infighting may result in another mass campaign.

## *Lack of career advancement*

Students often complain about the lack of equipment and dwindling funding for basic sciences, humanities, and theoretical social science in China. A survey of returned students in China in 1989 listed obstacles to research (in order): lack of funding, lack of information, bureaucratic inefficiency, distractions of daily life, and lack of scholarly partners. They are afraid that they will not be allowed to attend international conferences which would help them keep up-to-date in their research.[5] Chinese universities and state offices do not have enough room to take all of the Chinese graduates, much less all the graduates from the United States if they did return. The government's promise to improve the academic situation has often gone unfulfilled.

## *An easier, more fulfilled life in North America*

Many students have come to believe in the American Dream. Most enjoy a higher standard of living than they could expect in China where housing is scarce and some families who return have to split up and live with relatives. In China, academicians live on fixed salaries from the government, so they have to moonlight in order to make ends meet in inflationary times. Being able to work in a more "pure" research environment in the United States also has great appeal.

## *Their children have become Americanized*

While some parents delayed their return to China to see if

conditions would become more favorable, the children became "Americanized" - unwilling to study hard or to study Chinese. If the family returned to China their children would lag behind in mathematics and science skills and would do poorly in the national examinations that determine who will enter Chinese universities. Some parents sacrifice their own desires to return for their children's future. Some plan to go back to China once their children enter American universities.

## Families and research institutes encourage them to stay in the United States

Returning to China brings shame to their families because people in China think that returnees are losers when everybody is trying to leave. The family often had given their savings to get their children out of China. Though some want to return, their desire goes against the strong current of "going abroad." Colleagues in research institutes counseled those in the United States to stay, partly because they do not want to share their small budget with anyone else.

## Problems with reentry/ reverse cultural shock

Those who have gone back for short visits have been surprised by the radical changes in China while they were away for five to eight years. They often get lost in their home cities because of all the commercial development. Others do not know how to talk with old friends who have moved up social or political levels. Everyone seems obsessed with making business connections, rather than friendships, in order to succeed at "getting rich is glorious." The rise of traditional or superstitious behavior, such as *fengshui* or fortune telling, makes others uncomfortable.[6]

## *Losing hope for China's future*

Some students and scholars have wondered whether any political change is possible in China. Is the country "stuck" in its cultural problems? Critiques of Chinese culture in the last decade have included the television miniseries *River Elegy* (1988), Bo Yang's *The Ugly Chinaman* and Sun Longji's *The Deep Structure of Chinese Culture*.

## *New Christians know only an American setting*

Some of those who have become Christians in the United States do not know much about the history of the church in China. Those who know more may fear they would be unable to maintain spiritual and intellectual freedom if they return to China. They may wonder if they will be able to find a suitable place for fellowship. Others fear that they may not advance in their jobs if their Christianity becomes known.

A survey of 273 Chinese students was taken between January and October 1993. Of those who were "leaning toward remaining in the U.S.," the following reasons were given (in order):

1. Lack of political stability

2. Lack of political freedom

3. Lack of opportunity for career advancement in China

4. Poor work environment in China

5. *Three way tie between* lack of opportunities to change jobs in China, living standard in China too low, and better opportunity here for children's future

6. *Tie between* lack of modern equipment for your research or work and fear of not being able to get out a second time

7. *Tie between* difficulty in getting out the first time and how people look on people who have returned as if they have failed.[7]

# Reasons Why Students and Scholars Return to China

## *They have to, due to visa limitations*

Visiting scholars often come on one- or two-year visas.

## *They are well-connected*

They may be sons or daughters of top or mid-level leaders who can make money in this era of unregulated business opportunities. Others benefit from connections through alumni groups.

## *They are entrepreneurs*

They have the skills, such as law, business and economics, to establish private law or consulting firms. They are also ambitious, committed, optimistic, and thick-skinned to survive in a rough and tumble place. Some find their own funding instead of competing with jealous colleagues.[8]

## *A glass ceiling for Chinese in the United States*

Others have experienced discrimination or impossible competition in the States, where their limitations in English language skills jeopardize their advancement. Some are tired of outperforming their peers but not receiving recognition from their superiors.

## *Failure to adapt to American life*

Some find that they are unable to compete for good jobs. Other feel insecure, never being at home in America. Older scholars have family obligations which draw them back.

## Government incentives

For ten years the government has promised start-up grants, returned student centers, securing transfers of resident permits, swift promotions, opportunity to run their own laboratories, and decent housing. Since everything in China depends on the local situation, some returning students are better off than others.

## Fewer jobs available in United States

Some companies have scaled back their basic research operations, such as IBM and Bell Laboratories.

## Patriotism

Some have hope that China can change and they feel they should do their part in building her future. For example, some believe education, democracy, science, and technology will bring the necessary change in the culture.

The 1993 survey gave reasons why someone might return (in order):

1. Higher social status in China

2. Patriotism

3. Better career opportunities in China

4. Family ties in China

5. Want to be involved in Chinese reform

6. Can make more money in China than United States/Canada

7. *A tie between* positive effects of Deng's "trip south" encouraging economic reform in January 1992 and better education for children.[9]

## Alternatives to Returning to China

One alternative is finding work in Asia. John Naisbitt, in his book *Megatrends Asia* (1996), wrote about the "Asia Connection." For example, Singapore needed engineers and was successful at setting up new research laboratories. It offered good salaries, similar language/culture, and was experiencing an economic boom. Hong Kong also had high salaries and a low tax economy. The new Hong Kong University of Science and Technololgy (built since 1990) had hired four hundred fifty scientists, engineers, and management specialists, 75% of whom were ethnic Chinese educated in the West.

Another alternative to returning is to participate in short-term visits as experts. Students can lecture on their fields of expertise, conduct joint research or do research, such as in social science. They see this as a way to strengthen China without losing their own freedom. For those who do return, some teach one semester a year overseas to supplement their meager income.

## Conclusion

Our friends' decision to return to China is a complex situation. Each alternative has great costs and benefits. Some experienced great heartaches when they found they did not fit comfortably in either culture and were not appreciated by either culture. May we offer wisdom and compassion in our conversations.

# For Further Reading

John Naisbitt, *Megatrends Asia* (New York: Simon and Schuster, 1996)

Kyna Rubin, "At Home Abroad," *International Educator*, Winter 1995, 16-19.

_____, "Out of the Cultural Revolution: Chinese Faculty Blossom in America," *International Educator*, Summer 1994, 13-15.

Su Xiaokang and Wang Luxiang, *Deathsong of the River: A Reader's Guide to the Chinese TV Series Heshang*, trans. Richard W. Bodman and Pin P. Wang (Ithaca, NY: Cornell University East Asia Program, 1990).

Sun Lung-kee, *Zhongguo wenhua de "shenceng jiegou"* (The "Deep Structure" of Chinese Culture) (Hong Kong, 1983). Only in Chinese.

David Swinbanks and Elisabeth Tacey, "Chinese Scientists Drawn Back to Asia," *Nature*, Vol. 383, No. 6595 (Sept 5, 1996), 11-15.

Bo Yang, *The Ugly Chinaman and the Crisis of Chinese Culture* (North Sydney, Australia: Allen and Unwin, 1992).

# Notes

[1] Jim Mann, "China's Lost Generation," *Los Angeles Times Magazine*, March 25, 1990, 14-15.

[2] Geremie Barme, "Letter of Protest Opens Chinese Eyes," *Far Eastern Economic Review*, April 2, 1987, 38.

[3] Liu Binyan, *A Higher Kind of Loyalty*, trans. Zhu Hong (New York: Pantheon Books, 1990), 276.

[4] "NAFSA Study Mission to the People's Republic of China, October 20-November 3, 1987," 5; Jean B. Ringer, ed., "NAFSA Study Mission to the People's Republic of China, October 19-November 2, 1988," 6-7.

[5] Ruth Hayhoe and Sun Yilin, "China's Scholars Returned from Abroad: A View From Shanghai, Part Two," *China Exchange News*, Vol. 17, No. 4 (Dec. 1989), 6.

[6] Zhou Min, "Home is Where One Starts From: Reflecting on the Lessons of Re-entry," *China Exchange News*, Vol. 24, No. 1 (Spring 1996), 16-17.

[7] David Zweig and Chen Changgui, *China's Brain Drain to the United States: Views of Overseas Chinese Students and Scholars in the 1990s* (Berkeley, CA: Institute of East Asian Studies, University of California, Berkeley, 1995), 123.

[8] Kyna Rubin, "Homeward Bound," *Far Eastern Economic Review*, May 18, 1995, 74-75; Kyna Rubin, "Some Chinese Students Head Home," *NAFSA: Association of International Educators*, Vol. 46, No. 6 (April/May 1995), 1.

[9] Zweig and Chen, 123.

# Imparting a Vision of the Kingdom of God:
## The Challenge of Discipling Chinese Intellectuals

*Stacey Bieler*

In order to remain faithful and joyful Christians throughout their lives, Chinese Christians need to gain a vision of God's rule and their role in His world. Proverbs 29:18 challenges us with the importance of having that vision: "Where there is no vision, the people perish." We can prepare students and scholars to "live a life pleasing to God" whether they settle in China, North America, or Asia.

When considering whether to return to China, our Chinese Christian friends often fall near one of two ends of a continuum.

| Fearful of China's political system | ←——→ | Naive about Anti-Christian discrimination |

Some fear the political power struggles in China and do not see how God could work through them to build the kingdom of God if they returned. Many who stay in North America are thankful that politics do not affect every area of life. They take advantage of the situation by only worrying about their own personal success. At the other end of the spectrum are those who are uninformed about the history of suffering of the church in China since 1949. When they return to China they may be surprised by the lack of freedom and end up discouraged and immobilized in building God's Kingdom. The first group *begins* discouraged and the second group *becomes* discouraged!

If we impart a vision for the kingdom of God to our Chinese friends, we can provide an antidote for both extreme views. We can help each Chinese Christian student and scholar know both the power of God and how to be more wise about "being in the world but not of it."

Power of God as greater    ◄———►    Understand the actual
than any Ruler                          situation in China

While in North America, Chinese Christians have various opportunities to grow in their faith, but sometimes their faith remains superficial. Many attend weekly church services and Bible studies. Some have found that yearly conferences or Christian magazines help them to grow. A few look for ways to deepen their Christian walk. After a few years some soak up Christian values and are transformed. But other Chinese, who make professions of faith, do not grow and within five years are no longer active in any fellowship. This is often because a firm foundation has not been built in order that their hearts and minds become transformed to conformity with Christ.

The following proposal which addresses aspects of Chinese culture and recent Chinese history is intended to provide such a foundation. The four themes are: (1) Extending the Kingdom of God, (2) Living in Community, (3) Learning to be a Servant-Leader, and (4) Having a Hope for Change. Our goal is to weave these four threads together in order to impart a vision of spirituality and service that will sustain Chinese Christians through the rest of their lives. (This is not a replacement for a chronological study of the Bible, but a complement which addresses the background and needs of Chinese students and scholars).

The process of helping Chinese understand their role in God's world can be in a one-on-one relationship or small group study. Scholars, who only stay one or two years, and students, who have heard God's call to return to China, may recognize their need more than those who are planning to stay in North America. The earlier a student catches a vision of God's kingdom in their academic life, the better they can practice incorporating God into their studies. It may be more difficult to convince students of their need if you wait until their last year when they are writing and defending their dissertations *and* applying for jobs or post-doctoral positions. While Appendix A outlines a one year plan, Appendix B offers various Bible studies, books, and movies as resources.

## Extending the Kingdom of God

Our Chinese friends' worldview is the sum total of their cultural, social, and political assumptions about the world. Though they may have rejected Marxism and are searching for something else to fulfill their lives, it still colors the way they look at the world. Their focus has been on this world: what one sees is *all* there is, the only thing that is "really real." They consider those who believe in God as superstitious. Confucius' view of human nature, that people are perfectible through education, has caused many Chinese to be overly optimistic. After Tiananmen Square in 1989, many Chinese became Christians because only Christianity clearly explained the evil they witnessed: people are sinful and selfish.

When we become Christians our view of the world and our place within it changes. In *The Gospel of the Kingdom*, George Ladd describes the tension inherent in living during these in-between times.

←— Creation —— Jesus' first coming ____ Jesus' second coming —→
as Savior                as King

The kingdom is both present *today* because of Jesus' incarnation, but it is also coming *tomorrow* when Christ returns as reigning King. Having a well-developed view of the kingdom *today* gives us courage to work now. Understanding that the Kingdom is coming in its fullness tomorrow helps to keep us humble and prayerful, knowing that God has the ultimate victory. As Ruth Siemens has said, "The war is *over*. The Victor is known. We are the mop-up crew who are still fighting small battles because the Loser is unwilling to admit defeat." It is *not* a dualistic view where the outcome is uncertain. Isaiah 2: 2, 4 describes "In the last days the mountain of the Lord's temple will be established as chief among the mountains; It will be raised above the hills, and all nations will stream to it. . . [God] will judge between the nations and will settle disputes for many peoples. They will beat their swords into plowshares and their spears into pruning hooks."

Irina Ratushinskaya is a Russian poet who was arrested and imprisoned in a Soviet labor camp for four years during the 1980s. Her crime was writing poetry. Her memoirs, *Grey is the Color of Hope*, tells of her life with other inmates who were also arrested for "political crimes against the state." She thanked Alexander Solzhenitsyn for his priceless counsel, "Never believe [the guards], never fear them, never ask them for anything." She wrote that the best way to retain one's humanity in the camp was by caring more about others' pains than about one's own. She warned that if prisoners allowed themselves to hate, "it will flourish and spread during your years in the camps, driving out everything else, and ultimately corrode and warp your soul." One of her fellow prisoners told how her grandmother had responded to a government's decree that they would remain in "eternal exile." She smiled, saying, "They think that they are masters of eternity?"[1] After Irina was released, she arrived at her home and invited the KGB official in for a cup of coffee. He declined and left. She wrote,

"What of it, that I offered a KGB man a cup of coffee? I am the victor, not he!"[2] Steve Taylor, an English poet, wrote a poem for Irina.

### Beaten But Not Lost

We beat her
and she lost weight.
She lost blood.
She lost consciousness.

But she never lost hope.
She never lost poetry.
And she was never lost.

You must have to beat real hard
to get the God
out of these people;
To still the noise of heaven
in their hearts.[3]

The "noise of heaven" in her heart sustained Irina through prison. Turner's poem is a reflection on 2 Corinthians 4:7-10, where the Apostle Paul says that we are "jars of clay." We are uncomfortable with this image because we do not like to be broken or think of ourselves as weak or fragile! But God wants to show the world that "this all-surpassing power is *from* God and not from us." Though hard-pressed, perplexed, persecuted and struck down, the apostle Paul says that we are not lost. We are not people without hope.

Though the world proclaims that personal power is the basis for strength, the Bible tells us that in "repentance and rest is your salvation, in quietness and trust is your strength" (Isaiah 30: 15).

Steve Taylor wrote "Psalm" to describe this kind of life.

Not my works
  but your work
Not my perfection
  but yours
Not my grasp
  but your grip
Not my completeness
  but yours.

Not my strength
  but your strength
Not my honesty
  but yours
Not my trust
  but your truth
Not my will be done
  but yours.[4]

Real power and strength comes as we submit to God's will and are led by His Spirit.

Since God is in control, each member of His family can work courageously and responsibly with Him to grow the Kingdom of God. This courage to work in Christianity is radically different from the ethic of other religions. In *The Gospel in a Pluralist Society*, missionary Lesslie Newbigin tells of a conversation where his learned Hindu friend said, "As I read the Bible I find in it a quite unique interpretation of universal history and, therefore, a unique understanding of the human person as a *responsible actor in history*. You Christian missionaries have talked of the Bible as it were simply another book of religion. We have plenty of these already in India and we do not need another to add to our supply."[5]

For a moment let's consider how we would feel if we thought the world was out of control. The protagonists in Walker Percy's novels are usually lapsed Catholics. In *Love in the Ruins,* the psychiatrist Dr. Thomas More, finds that his Jewish friend, Max, sees the world as much more comprehensible than he does.

> Here's an oddity. Max the unbeliever, a lapsed Jew, believes in the orderliness of creation, acts on it with energy and charity. I the believer, having swallowed the whole thing, God Jews Christ Church, find the world a madhouse and a madhouse home. Max, the atheist sees things like Saint Thomas Aquinas, ranged, orderly, connected up.[6]

No wonder Dr. More is both an outpatient *and* a doctor at the same mental institution! How we view the world makes all the difference in how we respond to it! Do we shrink from the challenges and wither in our hope or are we renewed daily by God's power and his concern for us and his world?

Finally, as we recognize Jesus' Lordship with our minds as well as our hearts, we need to be renewed so that we can "take captive every thought to make it obedient to Christ" (2 Corinthians 10:5). For over one hundred years, Chinese have believed that science, technology, democracy and education would create a strong and prosperous China. Many who become Christians still retain their hope in these worldly systems and only add God as a patina to the surface of their lives. It may take time for them to shift their perspective so that their trust is solely in God and their studies are dedicated to God as tools to accomplish His work. Students who have despaired that their degrees do not fulfill their dreams often can become strong Christians since they know Jesus as the *only* hope. James Sire's *Discipleship of the Mind* offers a list of books and professional organizations for most disciplines that will help them not to "conform any longer to the pattern of this world, but be transformed by the renewing of your mind" (Romans 12:2).

The Christian worldview gives us the foundation for understanding history and welcoming the future. It also provides a purpose for our lives and our work, challenging us to participate in God's greater work in the world.

## Living in Community

Since the 1920s Chinese have tried to free themselves from the authoritarianism of the Confucian family system. The Chinese Communist Party sought to substitute filial piety toward elders with allegiance to the Party. During the Cultural Revolution, families were splintered when political leaders demanded that members falsely incriminate one another. Our friends' memories of community in China can include manipulative leaders, broken relationships, and a society filled with people yet to experience true forgiveness.

The Christian life involves learning that we *need* each other. All Christians need to be part of a community that encourages us to pray, hope and continue to work for change in our neighborhoods and professions. From a lofty discussion of Christian worldview, we crash into the reality of living at peace with one another! Some Chinese, who have seen political leaders misuse their power, often resist trusting and submitting to others. We North Americans suffer from individualism and need to learn about the corporate character of our faith. Creating a healthy balance between community and individuality is a good antidote for all of us. Dietrich Bonhoeffer knew the need for both. In *Life Together,* he wrote two chapters entitled "The Day with Others" and "The Day Alone."

The apostle Paul used the image of the *family of God* for this community. In a family we learn to love one another, to forgive, and to be unselfish. Colossians 3: 12-14 summarizes many of these qualities.

> Therefore, as God's chosen people, holy and dearly
> loved, clothe yourselves with compassion, kindness,
> humility, gentleness and patience. Bear with each
> other and forgive whatever grievances you may
> have against one another. Forgive as the Lord
> forgave you and over all these virtues put on love,
> which binds them all together in perfect unity.

We can choose Bible studies that look at case studies of struggling churches (such as Corinth, Galatia or Philippi) or focus on the fifteen "_____ one another" (such as loving, forgiving, etc.) passages in the New Testament epistles. This life-long reorientation from individual selfishness to selflessness within community takes place as we daily choose to follow Jesus.

Paul also used another image, the *human body*, in which all the parts function together for the good of the whole. We recognize our dependence upon each other as we learn the joy and limits of using our own spiritual gifts and encourage others to use theirs. 1 Peter 4:10 says, "Each one should use whatever gift he has received to serve others, faithfully administering God's grace in its various forms." As we acknowledge that our gifts come from the Lord, we are thankful for the opportunity to serve others, and learn to receive His grace from others.

Exiles from the Chinese Democracy Movement who now live in the West have experienced much infighting among its self-promoting leaders. Some have turned to Christianity to learn more about how to work together.[7] Paul told members of the early church to focus on their similarities rather than the differences. Ephesians 4:4-6 says,

> Make every effort to keep the unity of the Spirit
> through the bond of peace. There is one body and
> one Spirit - just as you were called to one hope when
> you were called - one Lord, one faith, one baptism,
> one God and Father of all, who is over all and
> through all and in all.

235

Imagine what a difference this recognition of unity could make in our interactions with other Christians! As we remember that we all stand at the foot of the cross as forgiven and redeemed sinners, we can join together to proclaim His goodness and salvation to the world. Jesus is revealed to the world through a loving community. As part of His prayer for His followers (John 17:23), He asked His Father, "May they be brought to complete unity to let the world know that you sent me and love them even as you have loved me."

As our Chinese friends act as a family and as a body, the Chinese church will become a powerful witness in North America and in China. Once they have tasted the sweetness of being in fellowship they will seek to make connections with other believers wherever they live.

## Learning to be a Servant-Leader

In China's past the emperor's power was circumscribed only very weakly by Confucian scholars whose obligation was to remind the ruler that he lived to serve his people, not himself. When the ruler did not want to be reminded of this, he would banish his scholar-advisers. In recent history, intellectuals who have criticized the government have often been banished to the countryside or imprisoned. In the late 1980s some hoped that a Chinese leader would emerge who was enlightened enough to listen to advisors and to be fair to the people. Tiananmen Square convinced many of the truth that "absolute power corrupts absolutely," and that none could be trusted to be a wise and just leader.

Leadership as servanthood is a startling new concept to Chinese and needs to be modeled and practiced to be convincing. Even those around Jesus had difficulties in choosing such a pattern. In response to a dispute among the disciples as to who was the greatest, Jesus said, "The greatest among you should be like the youngest, and the one who rules like the one who serves. I am among you as one who serves" (Luke 22:26-27). Steve Taylor's song, "Hero," tells of a young boy who wanted to be a hero, but had been disappointed by those he had idolized. However, one night

> When the house fell asleep
> from a book I was led to a light that I never knew
> I wanna be your hero
> And he spoke to my heart from the moment I prayed
> here's a pattern I made for you
> I wanna be your hero.[8]

Jesus' pattern requires a reorientation of the methods and goals of leadership. Look at the stark differences that George Malone presented in *Furnace of Renewal*.[9]

| Secular Authority 'Lord over' | Servant Authority 'Servant Among' |
|---|---|
| power base | love/obedience base |
| gives orders | under orders |
| unwilling to fail | unafraid/model of transformation |
| drives like a cowboy | leads like a shepherd |
| needs strength to subject others | finds strength in submission |
| authoritarian | steward of authority |
| has gold, makes rules | follows golden rule |
| seeks personal advancement | seeks to please master |
| expected to be served | expects to serve |

How can this reorientation happen at our deepest soul level? Besides studying the life and teaching of Jesus, we can look at other people in the Bible. Moses was overburdened until he learned to delegate. Nehemiah had to deal with opposition within and without his group. Paul confronted his congregations in tears. And Timothy felt the insecurities of a young leader. Being introduced to one leader in the Bible such as Moses or Nehemiah may allow students to mine that life as a treasure for the rest of their lives.

One semester we studied the life of David in our international Bible study. In 2 Samuel 30:1-15, David and his men found out that their women and children had been captured and taken away by the Amalekites. David, the great warrior, did not rush off to battle. Instead he turned to God and asked what to do. The students were amazed by David's dependence on God even in his area of strength.

We can also learn from Chinese Christians who have responded with compassion and service in the midst of difficult times. In the first half of the twentieth century, Chinese students who returned to China faced poverty, disease, an unstable government, famine, an eight year war with Japan followed by tremendous inflation and a civil war. Despite these surroundings, they answered God's call creatively. For example:

## Mary Stone (Shih Meiyu, 1873-1954)

> She was born into a Christian family in central China. She received her M.D. from the University of Michigan in 1896. After raising money in Chicago, she returned in 1901 to establish the Danforth Hospital in Jiujiang, four hundred fifty miles up the Yangtze River. Her hospital had ninety-five beds, a convalescent ward, and a home for the handicapped. She trained five hundred nurses in

twenty years before moving to Shanghai and co-founding the Bethel Hospital and Mission.

## John Sung  (Sung Sanjie, 1901-1944)

He was a son of a Methodist pastor/evangelist in a village in Fujian province. Sung received his Ph.D. in Chemistry at Ohio State in 1926. He remembered he had initially come to the United States to go to seminary. He found that liberal Christianity brought a deadness in his soul. On his voyage home, he threw all his degrees overboard, except for his Ph.D. which he presented to his mother. He became part of the Bethel Band of evangelists and traveled throughout China. His ministry extended to Southeast Asia where he preached to large crowds, impacting many to trust in Christ and dedicate their lives for full-time ministry.

## James Yen  (Yen Yangchu, 1893-1990)

Yen became a Christian after meeting an inspiring missionary teacher. After completing a bachelors degree at Yale, Yen went to France in 1918-1919 to serve with the Y.M.C.A. among the Chinese laborers who were helping the Allied forces. After finding that they could not write letters home, he started teaching literacy using the most basic one thousand characters. In 1920 Yen received his M.A. in history from Princeton. From 1926 to 1937 he led the Rural Reconstruction Movement in Ding Xian (Hubei Province), which became a model that other areas of China emulated. He recruited American-trained men with Ph.D.s from Cornell to help offer appropriate agricultural technology. From 1949 until his death he directed rural reconstruction projects in the Philippines, Africa, Central America, and Southeast Asia.

Here are three possible responses: medicine, evangelism, and rural reconstruction. Where are China's greatest needs today? Who will say "no" to the strong pull of materialism and individualism and pray for God's guidance and commit themselves to serve in China despite the costs?

We can also look at people in recent history who have made or are making a difference in their country or in the world. Possibilities include Chinese church leaders such as the late Wang Mingdao or Pastor Samuel Lamb (Lin Xiangao) in Guangzhou. Others could be the Czech playwright-turned-politician Vaclav Havel, the former President of South Africa F.W. DeKlerk, former United States president Jimmy Carter, or the late Mother Teresa. None of these are perfect leaders, but learning who and what has guided their decisions during difficult times will be beneficial.

Literature also provides positive and negative models of leaders. In *Things Fall Apart*, Chinua Achebe tells of Okonkwo, a man who wants to become a clan leader, but hates showing any signs of weakness and has no patience with unsuccessful men. His pride and fear finally drive him to commit suicide. Those who desire power have weaknesses and face similar temptations. They need to learn ways to understand the seductiveness of power and protect themselves from misusing the power entrusted to them.

Finally, leadership is learned through practice. We can offer a "safe place" within the community to practice skills, such as leading a small group Bible study or a large group meeting, being a song leader, guiding a prayer group or giving a sermon. These roles may not match exactly their gifts or calling, but they can help our friends grow in new areas. Taking risks helps grow our trust in God and keeps us from being judgmental of others. Learning leadership can also come by taking part in service projects, such as working in homeless shelters, homes for pregnant teenagers, or Habitat for Humanity. During school vacations, many churches offer week-long opportunities in urban centers, rural Appalachia (in Southeast United States), or in cleanup after natural disasters. Behind the scenes activities, such as setting up, cleaning up, counseling, and deacon's work are opportunities that can help mold a leader. We learn to repent and rest in God rather than strive to gain honor from others.

Whatever positions of leadership our Chinese friends come to serve in through their professions and in their churches, learning servant leadership can encourage them to do all things with joy as a "servant of all."

## Having a Hope for Change

The Chinese Communist Party tried to create a "New Man," men and women who would be good and selfless, through surveillance, re-education campaigns and reform camps. People were forced to write long confessions as a way to bring a change of heart. As the political climate shifted, the categories of class struggle fluctuated. For example, people were viewed as good or bad depending upon their family backgrounds. This type of fluctuation led many to despair. The utopian dream of creating these new men and women failed tragically, destroying many in the process. Instead of increased humanitarian values, falseness and reluctance to admit mistakes were common results. [10]

Christians believe that individuals, families, and even cultures can change for the better through the *inward* working of the Holy Spirit when we receive new hearts from God. Various passages in the Bible attest to the fact that God *can* work the greatest miracle — changing our lives. When David asked God,

"Create in me a clean heart" (Psalm 51:10), he acknowledged that it would happen only by God's intervention. In Ezekiel 11: 19, God promised that He would give us a new heart, one that is flesh rather than stone. 2 Corinthians 5:17 tells us "If anyone is in Christ, he is a new creation; the old has gone, the new has come!" Philippians 1: 6 says God does not forsake us, but "He who began a good work in you will carry it on to completion until the day of Christ Jesus." When we realize how prone we are to continue in our sins, our changed lives *are* a miracle! As God reveals new levels of our sins, we find He is our *only* hope for change.

One of our friends' mother visited her for a year. When her mom first met American Christians, she thought they were kind because they were "nice people." But when she met Chinese Christians who were kind, she took Christianity more seriously because she saw that it could even transform Chinese people! She then began reading the magazine, *Overseas Campus*, written for Chinese seekers. Her daughter, who is not a Christian, acknowledged that her mother has become more forgiving and helpful.

Second, what we do affects our surroundings for bad or for good. We would like to think that we can be selfish or angry without affecting others, but it spreads like a cancer, disrupting our relationships. This idea is wonderfully captured in the Chinese movie, *The Story of Qiu Ju*. It is about a woman who wants an older official to apologize to her, but he refuses. In comparison, Langdon Gilkey remembers how one man, Eric Liddell, portrayed in the movie *Chariots of Fire*, made a difference in a prisoner of war camp in China during World War II. After two years, the teenagers in the camp were out of control. Eric and other missionaries devised a program of evening entertainment.

> [It] was Eric's enthusiasm and charm that carried the day with the whole effort. Shortly before the camp ended, he was stricken suddenly with a brain tumor

and died the same day. The entire camp, especially its youth, was stunned for days, so great was the vacuum that Eric's death had left. There was a quality seemingly unique to the missionary group, namely, naturally and without pretense to respond to a need which everyone else recognized only to turn aside. Much of this went unnoticed, but our camp could scarcely have survived as well as it did without it. If there were any evidences of the grace of God observable on the surface of our camp existence, they were to be found here.[11]

We all need grace in our daily lives. A Malaysian returned student, who serves as a director within the Ministry of Trade and Commerce in Malaysia, tells about the impact of good relationships.

I have come to the conclusion that the only valuable theory of change is one of integrity. Whoever espouses such a theory needs to live by it and when you do that you have set up a model for moral leadership where people will begin to trust what you say, buy into your vision, get excited with the vision and make it their own. They too become agents of change. The Christian vision is the only vision I've seen to work.[12]

Others will pick up our vision. Kindness, selflessness, and integrity can spread, bringing a "fragrance of life" to all who are near (2 Corinthians 2:15).

We must not underestimate the results of our actions on society. Madeleine L'Engle's stories are captivating because the consequences of her characters' choices are not avoided. Movie directors have been interested in making a film of *The Arm of the Starfish*, but they want her to sign a contract agreeing that they can change the ending so it will be happier. She won't because she can't.[13] Our choices have consequences. God can redeem the circumstances (Romans 8), but we still have to live with the consequences.

Can our hope in God sustain us in the face of evil, personal failure and despair? Hope based on God's character and Jesus' work is the kind of hope both we and the world need. We have a "hope that does not disappoint us" (Romans 5:5). We, like the persecuted Christians in Asia Minor, should be ready to "give answer to everyone who asks you to give the reason for the hope that you have" (1 Peter 3:15). As we wait in anticipation of God's kingdom being fully established, God entrusts to us a mandate which gives our lives purpose. He has also given us the Holy Spirit who empowers and guides us to follow in His ways and to work for eternal rather than temporary rewards.

## Conclusion

Being part of such a small group will cost us time and energy. We will be investing in long-term commitments as we build these trust relationships. We risk having our own weaknesses and strengths become more apparent as we grow close to others in the group. We will see areas in our lives that need change and will need others to pray for us. We will be stretched in new ways and we may fail.

It will also cost us our control. In *Reaching Out*, Henri Nouwen writes about providing a hospitable place where people can learn.

> [T]eaching, from the point of view of a Christian spirituality, means the commitment to provide the fearless space where such questions [why we live and love, work and die] can come to consciousness and can be responded to, not by prefabricated answers, but by an articulate encouragement to enter them seriously and personally. We cannot change the world by a new plan, project or idea.[14]

We will learn new lessons of dependence on God as we pray with confidence to God to conform our hearts and our friends' hearts to His will. Thankfully we know He will "do immeasurably more than we ask or imagine, according to his power that is at work within us" (Ephesians 3:20).

In closing, let us consider again the continuum between being politically frightened and politically naive which was introduced at the beginning of the chapter. In James Boice's *Two Cities, Two Loves: Christian Responsibility in a Crumbling Culture*, he describes how we become responsible rather than fearful, and realistic rather than naive.

> The Reformers did not see [the restoration of society] as something to be realized in history now, as if the efforts of God's people will culminate in their creating the new Jerusalem on earth. But a *vision* of the heavenly city gave them ideals for what might be done now and, at any rate, encouraged them to keep working optimistically, knowing that God guarantees that the end result *will be good and not evil*. The result of the Reformation answer to the Christ-and-culture question was thus both responsibility and realism. It was responsibility to be in the world and work responsibly for its improvement. But at the same time it was also a realistic understanding that the world will remain sinful and corrupt until God's final restoration of all things.[15]

Chinese Christians can make a difference for the Kingdom wherever they live. Are we willing to partner with them so they can come to know God as their only strength and hope throughout their lives, so that we as co-workers can serve the risen and glorious King? "The politics of the kingdom of heaven is the politics of faith, hope and love: faith that confesses the risen Savior, hope that looks for his appearing, love that is inflamed by his sacrifice on the cross. Only the realism of resurrection hope can sustain the Christian as a pilgrim traveling home."[16]

Ken Medema's song describes the difference that "The Call" can make on our lives.

> Can you hear it down the ages
> Like a mighty trumpet sound
> A call to leave the night
> And step into the morning
>
> It's a call to joy and gladness
> In a world of war and pain
> and yet it sounds a note of danger
> And of warning
>
> It's a call to leave your treasures
> And your trinkets on the road
> It's a call to join the weeping
> and to bear the sufferer's load
>
> *Chorus*
>
> It's a call to live like fools
> By another set of rules
> Well, it's a call to take
> Your cross in hand and follow
>
> It's a call to love the stranger
> It's a call to live as friends
> In a world that says
> Good fences make good neighbors
>
> And it's a call to face the makers of
> Destruction and of war
> And to plead that we
> Put down those guns and sabers
>
> It's a call to death and dying
> It's a call to life and birth
> And it's a call to plant the seeds of love
> On barren earth

*Chorus*

I hear the music and it's callin' me
Come and be all that you were born to be
Oh if anybody would come after me
Take up your cross and follow

It's a blood-stained invitation
To a life of sacrifice
A call to walk the road
That leads from here to glory

It's a joyful expectation
Of the dawning of the day
When God shall write
The final chapter in the story

It's a call to be the lowly
And it's a call to be the least
It's a call to join the fasting
That shall lead to final feast.[17]

# Appendix A: A Potential Structure For a Year Long Program

| Fall Quarter | Winter Quarter | Spring Quarter |
|---|---|---|
| Faith Community Worldview | Faith Community Servant Leadership | Faith Community Hope for Change |

1. The four threads are not easily separated. Hope for change comes from believing the Christian worldview. Leaders need a community to lead!

2. Throughout the year, the faith community is the context within which the other three threads are learned. At the weekly meetings, you could do Bible studies about some aspect of Community, such as the Sermon on the Mount, or an epistle, or topics such as love.

3. Outside reading could be one book dealing with the theme for the quarter. At each monthly potluck, several chapters of the book could be discussed or compared with a movie with the same theme.

4. Research projects could be presented at the end of each quarter. For "Christian Worldview," each person can read one book about their field of study listed in the bibliography of *Discipleship of the Mind*. For "Servant Leadership," each member could research a person they admire, reporting on the person's source of motivation and how they have reacted to various crises. For "Hope for Change," they could keep a journal of their responses to participating in a Christian service project, such as a homeless shelter or Habitat for Humanity.

5. In order to know what aspects need to be emphasized, consider your own strengths and weaknesses and those you are inviting to join you in the adventure. Some may come with a better understanding of the heart (community), but weaker on the head (worldview) or vice versa.

## Appendix B: Resource List

### A Model Program

Steven Garber, *The Fabric of Faithfulness* (Inter Varsity Press, 1996).

Garber describes a program for Christian college students who live in Washington, D.C. for a semester. He gives us humble and wonderful insights into helping students, who having become disillusioned with American politics, are then encouraged to link belief with behavior for the long haul.

### Resource List

1. Christian Worldview

*Christian Beliefs* (IVP Bible Study)

Arthur Glasser, *Spiritual Conflict* (IVP Bible study)

*Grand Canyon* (movie: How is God's providence seen even if you don't believe in Him?)

Graham Greene, *Monsignor Quixote* (novel: compares Marxism and Christianity)

Donald Kraybill, *The Upside-down Kingdom* rev. (Herald Press, 1990)

George Eldon Ladd, *The Gospel of the Kingdom* (Eerdmans, 1959)

Tony Lambert, *The Resurrection of the Chinese Church* (OMF/Shaw Publishing, 1994)

Mars Hill Tapes. Call for sample, 800-331-6407. Reviews and interviews about books on modern culture, including education, philosophy, arts.

Lesslie Newbigin, *The Gospel in a Pluralist Society* (Eerdmans, 1989)

Walker Percy, *Love in the Ruins* (Avon, 1971)

*Places in the Heart* (movie: What really matters in life? Are all things ultimately reconciled in Christ Jesus?

Irina Ratushinskaya, *Grey is the Color of Hope* (Vintage, 1989)

James Sire, *Discipleship of the Mind* (IVP, 1990)

Glenn Tinder, *The Political Meaning of Christianity* (Harper Collins, 1991)

Dallas Willard, *The Divine Conspiracy: Rediscovering Our Hidden Life in God* (Harper San Francisco, 1998)

2. Community

Dietrich Bonhoeffer, *Life Together* (Harper and Row, 1954)

*Christian Community* (IVP Bible Study)

*Christian Virtues* (IVP Bible Study)

*Christ's Body* (IVP Bible Study)

*Crimes and Misdemeanors* (movie: What are the results of our sins?)

*Love* (IVP Bible Study)

Henri Nouwen, *Reaching Out* (Doubleday, 1975)

_____, *Wounded Healer* (Image, 1972)

*Searching for Bobby Fischer* (movie: Can you remain compassionate in a competitive world?)

John Stott, *The Message of Ephesians* (IVP, 1979)

_____, *The Message of the Sermon on the Mount* (IVP, 1978)

3. Leadership Models

David Aikman, *Great Souls: Six who Changed the Century* (Word, 1998) (Billy Graham, Mother Teresa, Aleksandr Solzhenitsyn, Pope John Paul II, Elie Wiesel and Nelson Mandela)

*Chariots of Fire* (movie: What choices did Eric Liddell make along the way to leadership?)

Chinua Achebe, *Things Fall Apart* (Heinemann, 1958)

*David* (IVP Bible Study)

*Dead Poets Society* (movie: how did the students respond to the teacher's leadership?)

Charles Hayford, *To the People: James Yen and Village China* (Columbia University Press, 1990)

*Howard's End* (movie: The results of a man who leads a contradictory life)

*Integrity* (Fisherman Bible Study)

Gary McIntosh & Samuel Rima, *Overcoming the Dark Side of Leadership* (Baker, 1997)

*Old Testament Kings* (IVP Bible Study)

*Sung Songjie* (booklet in Chinese available from Ambassadors from Christ)

John White, *Excellence in Leadership* (IVP, 1986) (about Nehemiah)

4. Hope for Change

*Amistad* (movie: How one person can make a difference) (rated R)

James Boice, *Two Cities, Two Loves* (IVP, 1996)

Jack Kuhatschek, *Hope: Your Heart's Deepest Longings* (IVP Bible Study)

Madeleine L'Engle, *The Arm of the Starfish* (Dell, 1965)

*Les Miserables* (movie, musical: How the kindness of one priest changes a man)

Vishal Mangalwadi, *Truth and Social Reform* (contact McLaurin Institute, 1-800-582-8541)

*Perserverance* (IVP Bible Study)

Eugene Peterson, *A Long Obedience in the Same Direction* (IVP, 1980)

Becky Manley Pippert, *Hope has its Reasons* (HarperCollins, 1989)

*Schindler's List* (movie: How a hard-drinking womanizer saved 1100 Jews during WWII) ( rated R)

*The Story of Qiu Ju* (movie: How unrepentence ruins relationships)

*Tender Mercies* (movie: How one person changes when he experiences God's love)

# Notes

[1]Irina Ratushinskaya, *Grey is the Color of Hope* (New York: Vintage, 1989), 10, 238, 260, 240.

[2]Ratushinskaya, 7.

[3]Steve Taylor, *The King of Twist* (London: Hodder and Stoughton, 1992), 30.

[4]Turner, 90,

[5]Lesslie Newbigen, *The Gospel in a Pluralist Society* (Grand Rapids, MI: Eerdmans, 1989), 89, emphasis mine.

[6]Walker Percy, *Love in the Ruins* (Avon, 1971), 101.

7Kyna Rubin, "Chinese Political Exiles as Christian Soldiers," *The Asian Wall Street Journal Weekly*, October 10, 1993), 16.

[8]From his albulm, *Meltdown* (Sparrow, 1984)

[9]George Malone, *Furnace of Renewal* (Downers Grove: Intervarsity Press, 1981).

[10]Bo Yang, "The Ugly Chinaman," in Geremie Barme and John Minford, *Seeds of Fire* (New York: Hill and Wang, 1988), 168-173.

[11]Langdon Gilkey, *Shantung Compound* (New York: Harper and Row,1966), 192. Gilkey used pseudoneums. Eric Ridley is Eric Liddel.

[12]Steve Garber, *The Fabric of Faithfullness* (IVP, 199 ), 114.

[13]*Walking on Water: Reflections on Faith and Art* (Harold Shaw Publishers, 1980), 182-186; Notes from "The Butterfly Effect," a week-long class with L'Engle at New College Berkeley, July 1987.

[14]Henri Nouwen, *Reaching Out* (New York: Doubleday, 1975), 54, 60.

[15]James Boice, *Two Cities, Two Loves: Christian Responsibility in a Crumbling Culture* (IVP, 1996), 151, emphasis mine.

[16]Edmund P. Clowney, "The Politics of the Kingdom." Mars Hill Reprint, 8.

[17]Ken Medema, "The Call," from album *Flying Upside Down*, Brier Patch Music, 1986.

# Contributors

Stacey Bieler, M.A. Michigan State University, was formerly staff and trainer at InterVarsity Christian Fellowship. She is the co-author of *China at Your Doorstep*.

Jonathan Chao, Ph.D. University of Pennsylvania, B.D. Westminster Theological Seminary, is president of China Ministries International.

Cun-fu Chen is professor at Hangzhou University and director of Christian Research Centre at Zhejiang University, Hangzhou.

Edwin C. Hui, M.D., Ph.D., M.T.S., is Associate Dean (Chinese Studies Program) & Associate Professor, Medical Ethics, Spiritual Theology, Chinese Studies at Regent College, Vancouver, B.C.

Samuel Ling, Ph.D. Temple University, M.Div., Th.M. Westminster Theological Seminary, is president of China Horizon.

Liu Xiaofeng, D.Theol. University of Basel, is editor-in-chief of *Dao Feng* (Logos and Pneuma) and academic director at Institute of Sino-Christian Studies (Hong Kong).

Ping Cheung Lo, Ph.D. State University of New York, Buffalo, is lecturer in the Philosophy and Religion department at Hong Kong Baptist University.

Katie J. Rawson, Ph.D. University of North Carolina at Chapel Hill, D.Miss. Fuller Theological Seminary, is regional training coordinator for international student ministry for InterVarsity Christian Fellowship's Southern California Region.